RESPONSIBLE TRAVELLER

A practical guide to
reducing your environmental
and social impact

KAREN EDWARDS

summersdale

THE RESPONSIBLE TRAVELLER

An Hachette UK Company
www.hachette.co.uk

Summersdale Publishers Ltd
Part of Octopus Publishing Group Limited
Carmelite House
50 Victoria Embankment
LONDON
EC4Y 0DZ
UK

www.summersdale.com

Printed and bound in China

Printed with soy-based inks on FSC paper

ISBN: 978-1-80007-388-3

FSC
www.fsc.org
MIX
Paper from
responsible sources
FSC® C016973

Substantial discounts on bulk quantities of Summersdale books are available to corporations, professional associations and other organizations. For details contact general enquiries: telephone: +44 (0) 1243 771107 or email: enquiries@summersdale.com.

CONTENTS

INTRODUCTION

For so many people around the world, travel is a way of life. It brings us face to face with environments, ecosystems and wildlife we would only otherwise witness in documentaries, teaching us just how complex and powerful the planet can be. By broadening our appreciation of unfamiliar cultures and learning about history from varied perspectives, we are able to better understand human nature and this extraordinary world we live in. Whether we choose to travel out of curiosity, as respite for the mind and body, or for an exhilarating and life-shaping adventure, travel can be a truly humbling, and rewarding, experience.

While many of us are fortunate to be able to travel, we can't ignore the fact that we are in the midst of a climate emergency and that our collective footprint on the planet is becoming deeper. In some regions, tourism can overwhelm local environments and infrastructure. Local residents can also be negatively affected, even forced out of their hometowns, by tourism.

In 2019, an estimated 1.47 billion passengers took international flights – and according to the International Air Transport Association, this number is projected to rise to 1.8 billion by 2030. With experts predicting that soon more people will be travelling than ever before, it's up to us – as individuals – to make better choices to look after our precious world.

The Responsible Traveller delves into the environmental and social effects of travel and tourism, offering achievable solutions on how to reduce our impact while on the road. Through examples and storytelling, it will address the effects of tourism on the climate, communities and wildlife – and highlight how small but meaningful changes to the way in which we travel can make an almighty difference to the people and places we visit. Empowered with this information, you will hopefully feel inspired to seek out the most environmentally conscious and ethical travel experiences – and, in turn, play a part in preserving our beautiful planet, and the life that thrives around it, for generations to come.

IT'S A
BEAUTIFUL WORLD

Isn't travel a wonderful thing? It takes us out of our homes, and our comfort zones, and propels us into the big, wide world – opening our eyes to the incredible life around us. Naturally, reasons for travelling vary from person to person. While some people crave a quick getaway or a city break to escape the pressure of everyday life, others travel because of curiosity and a desire to learn. For many of us, travel provides healing – and the chance to re-examine what is important within our own lives. It can help us to build resilience and discover endurance, assert confidence, overcome struggle and find wisdom through experience. More importantly, perhaps, travel can give us the time and space to truly understand our minds and bodies. It allows us to live in the moment – where we can revive our hearts and heads through rest or long, mindful walks, and engage ourselves with exploration, cultural learnings and beautiful vistas.

When we go with no agenda other than to explore, travel can be a freeing experience. It also gives us the opportunity for reinvention: where nobody knows us, we can be whoever we want to be. Today, that person may be flamboyant and bold. Tomorrow, we can be thoughtful and quiet, happy in our own company. In essence, we can be who feels right to us in that exact moment. The friendships we build on the journey may be short-lived, but they are often a powerful connection of likeminded souls – entwining dreams and experiences. We snapshot little moments that will forever beckon a knowing smile. Memories are made that will linger in the cobwebs of the mind for evermore. And, when the time finally comes to return home, we sometimes leave a part of our heart in the place we wandered. Yet, we find ourselves imbued with knowledge and hope to last a lifetime. It's true what they say, not all who wander are lost – but it can be utterly delightful to lose yourself for a while in this beautiful world.

WHAT IS
RESPONSIBLE TRAVEL?

As marvellous as travel can be, recognizing that there are negative implications to tourism, and that we contribute to this, is the first step toward becoming a more responsible traveller. Once we understand this, it will be easier to look at our own ways of travelling and make the small changes needed to be better travellers. While our experiences are, of course, important – so are those of the people and environments that welcome us. So, how can we provide them with encounters similarly positive to those we enjoy? We can start by reframing our purpose of travel. Rather than only centring ourselves in the narrative – "I'm going travelling because *I* need to escape" or "We've been busy and deserve this holiday" – try to envisage it as a joint venture between the visitor and the visited, such as "I can't wait to experience Sicilian hospitality and a delicious, locally-cooked meal" or "Coming face to face with humpback whales on our boat trip is a reminder that life on this planet is vast."

RESPONSIBLE TRAVEL CONSIDERS...

→ **The political climate of the place**
For example, are there any human rights abuses taking place or dictatorial regimes that are inadvertently being supported by your presence?

→ **The environmental impact**
Is the environment or wildlife being exploited to please tourists? Or are natural resources being altered or depleted to make room for tourists? If so, are there organizations that can ensure tourist expenditure goes toward conservation and good practice?

→ **The effect on surrounding communities**
In tourist hotspots, are local people being priced out of their homes to make way for tourism infrastructure? If so, are locals gaining from your expenditure? Is there a way to make sure your spending goes further into the community?

REFRAMING OUR VIEW
OF "DESTINATIONS"

Next, we must acknowledge and appreciate that the places we choose to travel to are not just potential "holiday destinations", but people's homes, identity, history and security. By carrying this thought with us wherever we go, we are empowered to see things from another perspective – that the place we choose to visit is not there to serve us. While there's no doubt the community will want us to enjoy our time and feel welcome, it is unrealistic to think every experience will be just as we expect. This might mean forgoing little luxuries and perfections we may be used to, like enjoying a steaming hot shower every day or relishing a particular brand of cereal for breakfast. Not everyone lives in the same way as us, nor does everyone want to. Accepting and, better still, embracing the varied lifestyles we come across is not only a respectful and considerate way to behave, but it also helps us to truly get to know the places we visit.

ACKNOWLEDGING THE PRIVILEGE OF TRAVEL

Did you know that, each year, it's estimated that only 6 per cent of the world's population travels by plane? With that statistic in mind, perhaps we can view our freedom to travel with more gratitude. To possess a passport that allows us to enter other countries and explore those surroundings is, undoubtedly, a privilege. To have the option to take time off work without having to worry about the financial burden is a privilege. To have the freedom and peace of mind to leave the security of our homes and have the courage to explore somewhere new is a privilege. This doesn't mean we haven't faced adversity, or that we haven't worked hard for our holidays; however, acknowledging our opportunities is another big step toward becoming a more responsible traveller. The truth is, the industry caters to the small percentage of us who are financially able, and fortunate enough, to travel regularly, so it's up to us to adopt a more sustainable way of travelling. We hold the power to push for change and create a more considerate industry for the planet and its people.

CHAPTER ONE

ADVOCATING FOR THE ENVIRONMENT

THE ENVIRONMENTAL IMPACT OF TOURISM

The American Journal of Environment, Energy and Power Research, published in 2013, states, "the negative impacts from tourism occur when the level of visitor use is greater than the environment's ability to cope with this use within acceptable limits of change." In other words, while we know tourism can be a major contributor to economic development, if the infrastructure around tourism isn't properly regulated and measured, there can be detrimental effects – including increased pollution, habitat loss, increased pressure on vulnerable species, depletion of natural resources (such as water), soil erosion and an increase in carbon emissions.

Transportation, at the heart of tourism, emits the majority of the industry's harmful carbon emissions. In 2018, global aviation, in particular, emitted approximately 1.04 billion tonnes of CO_2 – accounting for 2 to 3 per cent[1] of global carbon emissions and 3.5 per cent[2] of effective radiative forcing (warming).

So how does this information affect us as individual travellers? Unfortunately, there is no way to make tourism sustainable enough to avoid negative effects completely. Instead, we can implement measures of best practice while travelling to ensure our individual impact on our environment is minimal.

In this chapter we look at some of the more problematic environmental issues that can arise as a result of tourism, and the ways in which we can *all* attempt to counteract them. If enough of us choose to adapt the way we travel, we will show governments, policymakers, tour operators and local communities that prioritizing the environment and local populations over convenience is something the majority of travellers support. Such advocacy will encourage environmentally conscious infrastructure to be put in place, allowing tourism to thrive in the most ethical way possible.

[BEING CONNECTED
TO NATURE IS] VITAL
FOR HAVING THIS
HUMBLE RESPECT
FOR THE PLANET AND
ALL THE ANIMALS
WE SHARE IT WITH.

LIZ BONNIN

UNDERSTANDING THE CLIMATE CRISIS

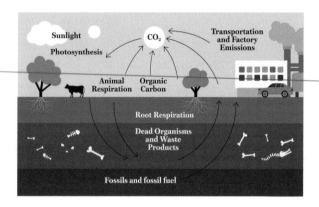

How does it work?

Many fixtures of modern life – including planes – rely on burning fossil fuels. The process generates greenhouse gases such as carbon dioxide (CO_2) and nitrous oxide (N_2O) and releases them into the atmosphere. Here, they absorb and trap radiation from the Earth's surface. Over time, this heat has contributed to our warming climate. Now, the Earth's average temperature has reached a crucial point, and if it continues to warm we will soon reach the 1.5°C average threshold above pre-industrial levels,[3] causing irreversible damage to large swathes of our environment.

WHY IT
MATTERS

IN THE POLAR REGIONS –
MELTING ICE CAPS

The Arctic is warming at a rate almost twice the global average.[4] The average temperature in Antarctica has risen by 3°C in the last 50 years.[5] As a result, polar ice caps and sheets – critical to the survival of marine wildlife such as polar bears and penguins – are melting. Ice also reflects radiation, so once it's gone, the ocean and Earth's surface will absorb even more heat – further adding to the problem. As water temperatures rise, some marine species will have to migrate to more suitable environments, which could completely unbalance ecosystems.

IN THE TROPICS – RISING
SEA LEVELS, FLOODING

As oceans warm, water molecules expand, causing a rise in sea levels. Coupled with the melting of polar ice and glaciers, the effect can be disastrous for coastal communities in the Pacific and Indian oceans, as well as low-lying deltas such as Bangladesh and the Nile. A 0.3-metre rise has already been recorded in the western Pacific, with a further rise of up to two metres predicted by 2100.[6] Millions of people are facing the terrifying prospect of displacement.

IN THE OCEAN – CORAL BLEACHING AND ACIDIFICATION

Corals are small, living, invertebrates that can take centuries to grow into the colourful reefs we see underwater. They play an incredibly important role in marine ecosystems, providing habitat, shelter, food and protection for countless species. As the oceans warm due to climate change, corals are coming under stress, which is causing them to expel the colourful algae that lives inside their tissues, a process known as "coral bleaching". This leaves the coral as colourless skeletons. While bleached corals are not dead, they are severely vulnerable – and many do die, which in turn stunts the growth of the reef. Furthermore, ocean acidification – caused by the absorption of increased carbon dioxide from the atmosphere – makes it harder for corals to build their calcium carbonate skeleton and form reefs. A 2020 report published by the Global Coral Reef Monitoring Network states that 14 per cent of the world's coral has been lost since 2009. Without reefs, entire marine ecosystems can collapse, destroying underwater habitats and exposing protected coastlines.

CASE STUDY:

MADAGASCAR IN PERIL

The island of Madagascar, located 250 miles off the coast of east Africa, has – for decades – faced the brunt of the changing climate. The fourth largest island in the world is home to thousands of endemic plants and animals with over 600 new species registered between 1999 and 2010. In August 2021, the United Nations confirmed the severity of Madagascar's plight, stating that the country was now facing the "world's first climate change-induced famine". In the south of the island, people have been experiencing their worst drought for 40 years – and their inability to farm is leading to poverty and displacement.

Speaking at the 26th Conference of Parties (COP26) summit in November 2021, Madagascar's environment and sustainable development minister, Baomiavotse Vahinala Raharinirina, described the desperate need for funding to build a pipeline to carry water supplies to southern communities. "There is a psychological distance to the problem. People see documentaries and pictures but do not feel it like we feel it," she explained. "People from the deep south of Madagascar are victims of something that they didn't do."

PLANES, TRAINS AND AUTOMOBILES

According to the 2019 United Nations Climate Change report, transport-related emissions from the tourism industry account for 5 per cent of man-made greenhouse emissions, and a whopping 22 per cent of global transport emissions.

Emissions by mode of transport[7]

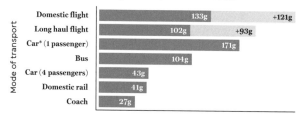

● CO₂ emissions

● Secondary effects from high altitude, non-CO₂ emissions

Mode of transport		
Domestic flight	133g	+121g
Long haul flight	102g	+93g
Car* (1 passenger)	171g	
Bus	104g	
Car (4 passengers)	43g	
Domestic rail	41g	
Coach	27g	

*Car refers to average diesel car

Measured by kilograms of emissions per passenger, per kilometre

We can see that a plane's emissions per passenger are highest by a distinct margin. Cars are also significant emitters, particularly when carrying just one passenger. By choosing to travel internationally and domestically by any other means of transport – including bus, train or coach – we can significantly reduce our individual contribution to carbon dioxide emissions.

Did you know?

A Eurostar journey between London and Paris emits up to 90 per cent less carbon than the equivalent plane journey.[8]

FLY, FLY, FLY AWAY (OR DON'T)

Passenger planes have, for over two decades, been classed as one of the fastest growing sources of greenhouse gas emissions. With more than an estimated 100,000 flights departing every day from airports across the world, aviation accounts for around 2.5 per cent of global emissions. As current measures stand, this is expected to *at least* double by 2050.[9]

While 2.5 per cent of global emissions might seem low compared to industries such as agriculture and home energy, it is a sizeable chunk to come from a small percentage of people. Remember, it's estimated that just 6 per cent of the population travels via plane, and many of those people are flying perhaps once a year or less, which means most aviation-related carbon emissions are caused by frequent flyers. So, our individual carbon footprint is greatly determined by how much we fly, and this is something we can only address as individuals. Of course, we don't have to stop travelling abroad altogether, but the number of trips we make – and planes we take – *does* matter and should be carefully considered as we tackle the climate emergency.

OFFSETTING EMISSIONS – DOES IT WORK?

WHAT IS CARBON OFFSETTING?

Offsetting starts with the consumer voluntarily calculating their carbon emissions using an online calculator. They then buy "carbon credits" for the same amount either via an airline or specialist websites. Those credits can then be donated toward global projects that endeavour to reduce the release of, or soak up, atmospheric carbon dioxide; for example by planting trees, creating wind farms, or supporting conservation programmes. The United Nations International Civil Aviation Organization (ICAO) also allows airlines and airports to offset aviation-related carbon emissions by purchasing carbon credits to make up for the energy they use.

IS IT RELIABLE?

While such schemes are well-intentioned, they do not negate the damage being caused by the concentration of carbon in our atmosphere **right** *now*. Experts even say planting the maximum number of trees would only absorb ten years' worth of carbon emissions at our current rate, and it would take nearly a century to do so. Additionally, reforesting and renewable energy can come with its own issues when not managed correctly, such as the use of non-native vegetation and monoculture plantations, as well as violations of Indigenous communities' rights.

So, how do we make more responsible choices when flying? While offsetting schemes don't cancel out emissions, they could be useful as part of the long-term solution to reduce carbon emissions. After all, if we can support enough well-managed reforestation projects, perhaps we will one day have healthy forests that can absorb more carbon dioxide in the atmosphere. With this in mind, it is still worth offsetting your emissions when possible.

Here's how to source a trustworthy offsetting scheme:

1. Prioritize *reducing* emissions first (see next page).
2. Choose a scheme that discloses exactly how "carbon credits" are used.
3. Support pre-existing rainforest conservation projects, where carbon is removed directly from the atmosphere.

→ www.climatecare.org helps to finance and manage global carbon reduction projects
→ www.greenr.co.uk works with shopping platforms to offset emissions
→ www.atmosfair.de works toward energy-efficient practices in the Global South

Travel industry experts are calling for a clear sustainability rating to be established for tourism experiences, so we can understand the true environmental impact of our trips.

LESS (FLYING) IS MORE

If you're someone who travels frequently, the best thing you can do is to take fewer flights as a way to reduce your environmental impact. Swapping domestic air travel for train or coach journeys – or attending business meetings by video call, rather than in person, is a great place to start. If you must fly, go direct – take offs and landings burn more fuel than cruising at altitude – and planning one long international trip, rather than multiple shorter holidays, also makes a big difference. Regular travellers will find their individual carbon footprint is generally heavier than those of people who don't travel by plane frequently, so any combination of these measures will make an effective difference.

Another consideration is to make small lifestyle changes at home, in between trips, to complement your desire to reduce your carbon footprint. For example, eating less meat and minimizing electricity and gas usage are great ways to be environmentally conscious every day.

OTHER WAYS TO REDUCE YOUR FLYING FOOTPRINT

CHOOSE PLANET-CONSCIOUS AIRLINES

Support the companies taking positive steps toward a sustainable industry. Air New Zealand and Cathay Pacific are using more fuel-efficient aircrafts and KLM has replaced old emissions-heavy 747 planes with twin-jet aircrafts. Look up airlines' sustainability policies for up-to-date reports.

BYO SNACKS AND REUSABLE WATER BOTTLE

Plastic packaging, water bottles and plastic utensils are the norm at airports and on planes – but can you imagine the tsunami of waste left behind? Carry reusable wooden cutlery, homemade snacks and a refillable bottle to avoid single-use plastics.

FLY ECONOMY

Even if you can afford First or Business class, consider swapping to economy. Premium cabins take up more space per seat, meaning fewer people can fit on each flight. The less the demand for premium services – where large amounts of emissions are being released to transport fewer passengers – the better.

TAKING THE TRAIN

While it may not always be the fastest or the cheapest mode of transport available, long-distance train travel is a great alternative to flying. Listening to the rhythmic clickety-clack of the wheels against the line, as you are gently rocked back and forth for hours, is almost meditative – and having the time and space to peacefully take in the changing landscapes outside the window can be a positively mind-whirring, therapeutic experience. There's also something physically, and metaphorically, liberating about train travel that isn't present during an airborne journey. There are no seatbelts holding you down and you are free to roam through the aisles at any time – generally without having to clamber over a stranger to do so. Chatting to fellow passengers feels more accepted, and there are stops every so often where faces and voices changeover – and where you can disembark whenever you wish. Best of all, perhaps, is the knowledge that travelling by train is a more planet-friendly way to explore – and by choosing this option, you're doing better by the world around you.

BE INSPIRED BY THESE FIVE CROSS-COUNTRY TRAIN JOURNEYS

THE CALEDONIAN SLEEPER

With double beds and en-suite bathrooms, the UK's Caledonian Sleeper is a relaxed way to travel overnight between London and Edinburgh or Glasgow, with the Highlander route connecting Aberdeen, Fort William and Inverness.

THE COAST STARLIGHT

On-board buskers provide the soundtrack to this journey along America's western spine from Seattle to Los Angeles – showcasing a patchwork of Pacific views and serving the nation's best-loved food, from enchiladas to fried chicken.

THE GHAN

Cutting through the Indigenous heart of Australia, this is a superb way to experience the continent's unique and extreme outback landscape between Adelaide, in the south, and Darwin, in the north.

THE GLACIER EXPRESS

Departing from Switzerland's Zermatt ski resort early in the morning, this journey takes in the iconic Matterhorn, Rhine Gorge and Rhône Glacier, before arriving at St. Moritz eight hours later.

THE ALASKAN RAILROAD

With a backdrop of snow-topped peaks, glaciers and seemingly never-ending alpine forests, you can spot moose, caribou and golden eagles on this mesmerizing three-hour ride from Alaska's capital, Anchorage, to the coastal city of Seward.

TO CRUISE OR NOT TO CRUISE?

The cruise industry is under constant scrutiny due to poor environmental practices. Larger cruise ships, in particular, have a bad reputation for endangering marine mammals, contributing to air and water pollution, adding to the destruction of coral reefs and causing the erosion of coastal regions by anchoring. They also often contribute to the negative effects of overtourism – such as the degradation of local environments and over-pricing of facilities for those living in cruise hotspots. If you choose to cruise, do it in a more considered way:

→ Select small ships for minimal environmental and social impact.

→ Pick a cruise line with a genuine sustainability policy – for example, Ecoventura operates naturalist-led, carbon neutral Galápagos Islands cruises, while Peregrine Adventures bans single-use plastics and sources 90 per cent of food from local producers.

→ Book with a cruise line that is registered with an environmental regulator, such as The Association of Arctic Expedition Cruise Operators (AECO).

→ New ships are likely to be more energy efficient; refer to their sustainability policy to confirm this before booking.

CASE STUDY:

BARCELONA'S BOOMING CRUISE INDUSTRY

In summer 2019, Barcelona mayor Ada Colau pledged to limit the number of cruise ships coming into its popular Mediterranean port in a bid to tackle overtourism. The Spanish city had just been declared the most polluted port in Europe,[10] with high amounts of sulphur dioxide and nitrogen coming from cruise ships. In 2018, 12 million people[11] visited the city. It was home to just 1.6 million people at the time. Issues such as unaffordable housing, thanks to a rise in Airbnb and holiday rentals, left many residents threatened with eviction.

"The way of life for all Barcelonans is seriously under threat," wrote Colau. "Of course, the answer is not to attack tourism. Everyone is a tourist at some point in their life. Rather, we have to regulate the sector, return to the traditions of local urban planning and put the rights of residents before those of big business."

Did you know?
Venice has intermittently closed and re-opened its main canal to cruise ships, because of environmental degradation.

IS EXPEDITION CRUISING THE ANSWER?

Expedition cruises, on small cruise ships, focus on education rather than entertainment. Lecture presentations from qualified scientists and academics complement the travel experience, propelling discussions about environments and cultures. The same experts act as guides out in the field, sharing their knowledge during onshore excursions and small-group powerboat tours. On-board restaurants and shops are typically kept to a minimum – and emissions compared to those from larger ships are much lower. Still, it's vital to ensure your expedition cruise is booked with an environmentally conscious cruise line.

→ Choose a company that displays a transparent, responsible travel policy on its website, addressing on-board sustainability and environmental awareness, as well as strategies to reduce social impact.

→ Cruise lines range from comfortable to luxury. However, more luxurious ships are likely to emit more carbon emissions and struggle to maintain a successful sustainability policy.

→ Opt for local companies when possible.

→ A small passenger capacity will have less of a footprint and make the experience more intimate.

DREAMING OF ANTARCTICA?

Whether you're coming face to face with nesting gentoo penguins, witnessing humpback whales feasting on krill or looking into the marble eyes of a Weddell seal as it lazes, full-bellied, on the ice, the Antarctic experience is mind-blowing and humbling all at once. The world's southernmost continent welcomes over 74,000 tourists each southern-hemisphere summer, mostly on cruise ships. Voyages to the region are regulated according to number of passengers by the International Association of Antarctic Tour Operators (IAATO). If you're hoping to visit this extraordinary and pivotal environment, please recognize that fully sustainable tourism isn't possible here. Instead, aim to travel in the most considerate way.

→ Avoid luxury or large cruise lines. Choose expedition companies that carry fewer passengers (under 200 is best, fewer than 100 is even better).

→ Book expert-led, conservation-focused expeditions.

→ Prepare for IAATO's strict biosecurity measures by ensuring all outerwear is cleaned and free of grass, mud and stones before you travel.

→ Consider visiting by sailing ship, which has a much smaller carbon footprint and environmental impact.

INTO THE WILD

Witnessing wildlife in its natural habitat can be one of the most rewarding experiences while travelling. There's something incredibly life-affirming about stepping into the world of another animal to watch as it interacts with other wildlife, completely unbothered about the presence of humans. Now a 250-billion-dollar industry, wildlife encounters are in high demand. As social media has grown, getting as close to the action as possible has become an additional requirement, and some operators feel pressured to chase and surround animals for that "Insta-worthy" photograph. While this might seem shocking to discerning travellers, these kinds of actions are increasingly common. The result can be a change in animals' behaviour, which might see entire families pushed away from an otherwise safe habitat. Some are even forced to abandon their young out of fear. For so many reasons, it's crucial to plan wildlife encounters with a trained, reputable and ethical operator, who will always prioritize the safety of the animals.

WHAT TO LOOK FOR IN AN ETHICAL WILDLIFE TOUR OPERATOR

The following tips will help you choose a wildlife experience that enforces responsible practice. Aim to tick off at least five of these points before booking.

→ Experiences led by wildlife experts who have studied a specific environment or animal.

→ A conservation-led manifesto that shows the operator cares beyond making a profit.

→ Family-run or locally-based operators who also take pride in their community and surrounding environment.

→ Tours that do not go to tourist-flooded regions, opting for lesser-known areas to avoid overwhelming the wildlife.

→ A clear policy on how they operate around wildlife displayed on their website.

→ Small-group tours that do not pack as many people in as possible.

→ Companies that maintain strict distances when in the vicinity of wildlife.

→ A trained operator who has history in the region and insight into the behaviour of the wildlife.

→ Information-based tours that teach you about the animals, rather than simply going in for a photo opportunity.

→ A genuine passion for wildlife and the environment in which it lives.

FIVE WILDLIFE EXPERIENCES TO BLOW YOUR MIND

COME FACE TO FACE WITH GREY WHALES

In the tropical bays around California and Baja California, breeding grey whales often become playful around boats, sometimes opening their mouths wide enough for witnesses to see the baleen in their upper jaw.

MEET THE MOUNTAIN GORILLAS

With just 1,000 mountain gorillas remaining in the equatorial African rainforest, limited trekking permits, to find gorilla families, are issued to visitors in Rwanda and Uganda each day. A portion of the revenue goes toward anti-poaching units and conservation.

PUFFINS GALORE

The UK's west coast is teeming with seabirds and marine mammals. Puffins and gannets, Atlantic grey seals, common dolphins and harbour porpoise can be seen at various times of the year.

BEAUTIFUL ORANGUTANS

Searching for orangutans in the Bornean and Sumatran rainforests with conservation-led operators provides much-needed support to protect this critically endangered species from habitat loss and poaching.

BROWN BEARS CATCHING SALMON

Photographic expeditions into Alaska's national parks can bring you close to caribou, moose and bald eagles. In summer, it isn't unusual to find brown bears, and their cubs, catching salmon from rivers.

THE MAGIC OF SAFARI

Whether exploring the jungles of Asia, deep in the savannahs of Africa, or diving into the rich and diverse waters around the world, the wildlife safari experience can be life changing. Here are a few extra tips to consider when planning and executing an excursion.

→ Choose a time of year to visit that doesn't coincide with high season.

→ Email the operator to ask about their ethics around the animals if you are unsure.

→ If you are choosing an experience where you can be in the water with the wildlife, ensure food isn't typically used to coax the animals, as this can interfere with their natural diet and encourage the association of food with humans.

→ Minimize noise to avoid frightening animals.

→ Never touch the animals or encroach on their personal space.

→ If your vehicle driver or boat captain chases the wildlife, ask them to stop, stating clearly that you don't condone putting the animals under stress.

WHY BOOK A CONSERVANCY?

Across the continent of Africa, nature conservancies have been set up to preserve land and resources, with hope this will also keep endemic wildlife populations safe and healthy. Conservancies are particularly valuable in tourist-heavy safari regions such as Botswana and Kenya, helping to preserve natural migratory passages, which can otherwise get uncomfortably overcrowded during the peak summer and winter seasons. Conservancies limit the infrastructure and number of guests able to stay within their borders and offer more sustainable accommodation options to those who do come. In turn, the safari guides are typically hired from the local community, sometimes lured away from a poaching background, which encourages more young people to train in environmental conservation. Guides have not only studied the wildlife but have often shared the same environment as the animals for years, so their observations, recollections and awareness bring so much to a safari experience.

KNOW YOUR LINGO

The Bantu language of Swahili is most commonly used in East Africa, although around 98 million people speak it across the African continent, including in Southern Africa. We use a few Swahili words in English too, which you may hear used with local dialects while out on safari.

"Hujambo" or "Jambo" is a friendly way to say "hello, how are you" in Swahili

Safari translated from Swahili means "an overland journey or hunt".

"Simba" in Swahili means lion.

A gracious "Asante" means "thank you"

CASE STUDY:

ELEPHANT CORRIDORS

Elephants are natural migrants. They move on to more favourable areas as the seasons and resources change – adapting to new environments as they go. This allows the animals to find fresh vegetation and helps heavily grazed regions to recuperate. Migration also encourages elephants to breed with other groups, diversifying the gene pool and broadening support and knowledge between family groups. Unfortunately, the large barrier fencing found on agricultural farms can isolate whole regions, preventing elephants from migrating along natural corridors. Conservancy managers understand the importance of such wildlife corridors and work hard to protect them by buying land, removing fences and preserving the natural environment. By donating to or staying at established conservancies, we can greatly help each region's migrating species and their habitat. In return, travellers are typically guided by knowledgeable local guides who hold a deep understanding of their environment.

THE WILDLIFE
EXPERIENCES TO AVOID

✗ ELEPHANT "ORPHANAGES"

Elephants found at many so-called orphanages and sanctuaries are often captured when young, typically after the mother is maimed or killed. Once captive, they are kept in small cages, their feet chained, with barely enough space to turn around. Their spirit is "broken" through an exercise known as "pajan", which involves starvation and being beaten into submission. A long stick with a hook at the end is used to dig into their flesh if they "disobey" commands. The ones that survive are used for entertainment – tourists are allowed to stroke, feed, bathe and ride them – with that hook never too far away.

✓ WHAT TO LOOK FOR IN
AN ETHICAL RESERVE

1. The goal of the orphanage should be to rehabilitate animals so they can be released back into the wild.
2. Elephants move freely, without restraints, and behave naturally without coercion.
3. Visitors can view the elephants at a safe distance, with no touching, bathing or riding.
4. No use of hooks or unpleasant force by workers.

5. There should be no baby elephants and, therefore, no captive breeding.

✗ CUB PETTING AND LION WALKS

The background to this animal encounter is far from pleasant. Cubs are usually taken from their mothers at just a few days old, causing extreme stress to both the mother and the cub. Once her first cub is extracted, the mother is forced to breed again and again – a process similar to factory farming. This causes tremendous distress to her body; whereas a wild lioness would only reproduce every second or third year, mothers in this kind of captivity produce two to three litters a year. Cubs then tend to be whipped into submission for their human visitors, while larger predators, such as lions and tigers, are sedated during visits. Once they are too old for petting, walking and photographs, the animals are sold to the canned hunting industry and left to be killed by recreational hunters.

✓ WHAT'S THE ALTERNATIVE?

See them in the wild! You can't beat a safari with knowledgeable guides who can tell you everything about these incredible wild cats. You'll likely witness unbelievable documentary-style scenes too.

✗ SWIMMING WITH DOLPHINS AND MARINE WILDLIFE PARKS

Call it a "marine park" or a "sanctuary" – these are sugar-coated labels for a place of captivity. Traditionally, calves are the prime inmates because they are easier to train. The process of capturing a marine animal typically starts with a boat chase causing panic, confusion and distress. It ends in exhaustion and being caught in a net. The animal is then lifted into a tiny, windowless tank and transported – sometimes hundreds of miles – to their new home. If they survive the journey, they are then generally held in a confined space with minimal food, which can cause sickness and behavioural abnormalities. When it's finally time to entertain the crowds, they are released into large pools and suddenly fed rewardingly, with the understanding that there is work to be done.

✓ WHAT'S THE ALTERNATIVE?

Choose to see magnificent creatures in their natural habitat, with a trustworthy, conservation-focused marine expert who will teach you about the animals' real behaviour and characteristics.

✗ PERFORMING WILDLIFE

Trained animal performances, for human entertainment, go back centuries. Orangutans and chimpanzees dressed up in human clothing and serving drinks, elephants painting pictures, bears dancing to music – these are all experiences that can still be seen around the world today. The animals are usually plucked from the wild as babies and separated from mothers to ensure they can be "trained" more easily. They are then threatened by a sense of danger – by beating, starving, whipping and even the pulling of teeth. In addition, they are often tied, prodded, drugged and kept in small enclosures. Experiences where the animal's behaviour seems unnatural or forced, where they don't have a say in whether they partake or not, or where the display isn't educational to the waiting audience, should be avoided at all costs.

✓ WHAT'S THE ALTERNATIVE?

If you come across an unnatural wildlife performance, make a direct complaint and leave a public review warning other visitors about what the show entails. Instead, choose to visit a conservation-led zoo where animals are under no pressure to perform, or book a wild experience where the animals are safe in their own habitat.

CASE STUDY:

THE GREAT BIG SHARK MYTH

Cult films such as *Jaws* and *Open Water* perpetuate the idea that sharks are dangerous and angry creatures, determined to feed on unsuspecting humans. Sharks are, in fact, peaceful and shy animals whose curiosity and lack of understanding can lead to "attacks". Most species are under serious threat due to overfishing and culling for shark-fin soup – the latter being a disturbing practice where sharks have their fins removed, often while the animal is still alive. Once the carcass is disposed of, the fins are sold to parts of Asia, where they are dried and prepared so they can be made into an expensive delicacy. An estimated 100 million sharks are killed every year around the world,[12] and populations have decreased by 90 per cent in a few decades.[13]

Some species – such as hammerheads and threshers – are on the brink of extinction. Snorkelling and scuba-diving programmes run by experienced operators can dispel these myths and help people gain an appreciation for the marine world. This is an example of how tourism can provide much-needed education.

FOR THE SNORKELLERS AND SCUBA DIVERS

An estimated one million new divers are certified each year.

If you love being in the ocean, embarking on a snorkelling or diving trip can be a life-changing adventure. There are thousands of underwater experiences to entice people, but not all prioritize conservation of the ocean and its creatures.

BOOK THROUGH A GREEN-FINS-APPROVED SNORKEL OR SCUBA-DIVING OPERATOR

The Green Fins initiative, established by the Reef-World Foundation and the United Nations Environment Programme, teaches divers, snorkellers, the diving industry and coastal communities how to be more conservation focused. It promotes sustainable, ethical and transparent diving experiences – with coral reef protection at the forefront of its efforts. The 15-step Green Fins Code of Conduct helps operators fine-tune their sustainable measures and adhere to standards.

Are you a Scuba diver? Take the Green Fins (www.greenfins.net) refresher e-course to understand responsible diving.

HOTELS, RESORTS AND GREENWASHING

Before they even open their doors, many hotels and resorts can generate a large carbon footprint. From the construction of infrastructure around the lodging, to transporting supplies and the day-to-day running of the business, the whole system can be exceptionally energy-intensive – and that's without considering the original land that has been lost to development.

With travellers more aware of the environmental crisis, it is now almost a necessity for businesses to promote a planet-friendly ethos, with some hotels and resorts brandishing "green" stickers and eco labels to absolve their commitment to sustainable practice. Others nod toward the odd "eco-friendly" measure, such as "tell us if you do not want your towels washed every day". On closer inspection, however, many companies are investing more in marketing spin than on adopting real and effective sustainable methods. This falsehood is known as "greenwashing" – a term coined in the 1980s by environmentalist Jay Westerveld. Greenwashing covers up a multitude of unsustainable practices in a time when we critically need to address climate change, plastic pollution, air pollution, water shortages and habitat loss.

COMFORTABLE
AND CONSCIOUS

Don't be disheartened, though, as there are many accommodation options practising the environmental and social changes that they preach. To find them, look for a clear and direct sustainability policy on their websites – and if you're unsure, don't be afraid to ask for more information via an email or phone call. Address these five questions before booking:

1. Do they adopt sustainable measures, such as solar power?
2. Do locals make up a large majority of their employees?
3. Do they grow their own food produce? Are there composting facilities?
4. Is there a waste recycling system or a ban on single-use plastics?
5. Do they recycle grey water and / or sewage on site?

READ THE FINE PRINT

To find the most environmentally conscious accommodation, research is important.

When investigating, you might see Google's green eco-certified badge pop up against hotel names. While this service has the best of intentions, it could encourage greenwashing. Opt to read about sustainable practices directly from accommodation websites rather than relying on a Google stamp.

SWAPPING LUXURY FOR SUSTAINABILITY

While luxury hotels and resorts are great for relaxing, they tend to encourage overindulgence – meaning emissions and waste are often amplified. Simple, locally run facilities will generally be more planet-friendly.

B&Bs AND GUEST HOUSES

Locally owned and run B&Bs and guest houses are an intimate accommodation option, where you can get to know your hosts. Breakfast is usually prepared to order, meaning food waste is minimal, and gardens provide the opportunity to grow produce.

HOMESTAYS

Living under the same roof as locals is a deeply immersive experience and offers the chance to get to know the intricate nuances of life in any region. Cooking and eating together, with your host, is a great way of bonding – and, again, it saves greatly on food waste.

AGRITOURISM

An idea established in Italy in 1985, agritourism has proved hugely popular with sustainability-conscious travellers. This beautifully natural experience invites you to stay on family-run farms, and not only provides a roof over your head, but also invites you to pick your own produce, go foraging and cook with the owners.

SOMETHING ELSE
TO CONSIDER

BALANCING CONSERVATION
WITH SOCIAL IMPACT

Many hotels ask guests to specify if they need their bedding changed, or towels washed, every day. Of course, the environmentally conscious answer would be to say "no", but while this practice conserves energy and water, cleaning staff may depend on that work to earn a salary. A good balance could be to say no to daily servicing, but still give your room attendant a personal tip for their efforts.

THE BIG BUFFET PROBLEM

Food waste usually ends up in landfill, meaning all the water, energy and other resources that went into producing those meals are also wasted. Once decomposed, the waste produces methane – a greenhouse gas even more potent than carbon dioxide. Rather than contribute to the overindulgence with half and full-board options, budget a small amount each day for eating at local cafés and restaurants. You will likely be eating fresh, seasonal produce while contributing directly to the local economy. Find a moment to explain your reasons to the hotel management team, who might be encouraged to make positive changes.

FIVE WAYS TO BE A BETTER LODGER

1. **Act as your hosts do.** If people are generally indoors by a certain time, there is likely to be a reason for that – such as safety – or because the electricity generator turns off.

2. **Eat what they eat.** This will not only make it easier to source seasonal food, but will also reduce food waste, save on the energy needed to prepare a separate meal and cut down on cooking time for the kitchen staff.

3. **Be conscious of your surroundings.** If your host region experiences limited rainfall, water might be a precious commodity. Booking into a resort with swimming facilities and a spa probably wouldn't be a considerate thing to do.

4. **Prepare to disconnect.** The online world doesn't always carry the same importance everywhere, and there may be times when you aren't able to access your email or social media.

5. **Go with the flow.** Every region has its own way of life. Remain respectful and understanding if things don't happen exactly as you'd like them to.

CASE STUDY:

WATER TROUBLE
IN PARADISE

Pre-pandemic, when tourism in Bali was booming, visitors from all over the globe would choose this Indonesian island to escape their daily lives. Bali offers five-star resorts, spas and hotels, each providing soul-melting experiences – except they exist at the expense of the local community. Water is a valued commodity in Bali because frequent rainfall is not guaranteed, yet 65 per cent of the island's water goes toward facilitating tourism.[14] The use of swimming pools, spa facilities, golf courses, monsoon showers and fancy bathtubs, and the regular washing of linen, causes much of the problem. Meanwhile, an estimated 1.7 million people lack access to clean water and some residents have to contend with an irregular water flow. Rice farming also suffers due to a lack of irrigation. As tourism continues to grow, perhaps we could all reconsider our need for indulgence in natural resources.

SUSTAINABILITY CHAMPIONS

All around the world, governments and councils are choosing to adopt sustainable initiatives, such as conserving local wildlife habitats or investing in community infrastructure. Still, there's a lot of work to be done, and to encourage more places to take this path, we need to show the people in positions of power that travellers will come if they take on this approach. The more we choose to invest in the places making positive changes, the more governments, larger tour operators and chain resorts will realize they, too, need to step up – because there *is* a demand for better environmental consideration. So next time you plan a trip, look into the regions advocating for a more sustainable way of welcoming tourists. These are places we should visit, so that we know our hard-earned tourist cash is going into the places striving to do better in the midst of the climate crisis.

THESE FOUR NATIONS ARE ALREADY DOING THEIR BIT

BHUTAN

The Kingdom of Bhutan requests that all visitors pre-book trips for a set nightly rate of $250 per person, regardless of where they go and what they do. This includes a 37 per cent tax that goes directly toward improving infrastructure, healthcare and education systems.

SLOVENIA

Slovenia's Green Scheme provides a nationally recognized certification programme, where tour operators, hotels and restaurants who enrol follow a strict 11-step process and are promoted by the national tourist board.

COSTA RICA

Costa Rica is already generating 98 per cent of the country's electricity from renewable sources. In addition, 25 per cent of the land is already a declared conservation zone. While tourists can visit the national parks, specifically built boardwalks and pathways keep their impact to a minimum.

ICELAND

Having installed a selection of natural spring water stations around the capital, Reykjavík in Iceland encourages both tourists and residents to ditch plastic and embrace reusable products.

THE PLACES
THAT NEED YOU

When a region or a country goes through a disaster – for example, an adverse weather event or terrorism attack – there is an inevitable drop in tourism. The Covid-19 pandemic has also left many countries that are heavily dependent on tourism as a source of income struggling to recover. The result is often a decimated economy that can take years to rebuild. Travelling to an affected region is a way to turn travel into a positive, especially if you can make bookings through local operators, reserve community-run accommodation and ensure expenditure goes to local businesses. Not only will you be injecting some much-needed money into the economy, but you will likely experience the region in a rare, more natural state – not overrun by tourists. For this reason, room rates and in-country costs are also likely to be cheaper – ensuring both you and residents benefit from your visit.

→ In April 2019, terrorist bombers attacked multiple churches and a hotel in Sri Lanka. Less than a year later, the country closed its borders due to the Covid-19 pandemic. The resulting loss of economic income will leave the country recovering for many years.

→ Although prone to intense hurricanes, Vanuatu's 83 islands are rarely all affected by the same adverse weather event. Yet they all suffer from the fall in tourism when these events happen.

→ In Bangladesh, there are an estimated nine local jobs allocated for each tourist that visits. Covid-19 has had an immense impact on tourism, with people still struggling to rebuild livelihoods.

→ In 2017, Puerto Rico was hit by hurricane Maria, a storm known as the region's worst recorded natural disaster. With little direct assistance from the US, the rebuilding process is taking years.

→ Experts predict a one-metre sea level rise could leave the majority of the Maldives underwater by 2100. The archipelago will need to build an economy as strong as possible in order to help displaced communities resettle if necessary.

CHAPTER TWO

AN EDUCATION IN CULTURE

One of the most rewarding aspects of travel is meeting people along the way. At the very least, they might suggest the best places to see from a local point of view or teach us something about their way of life. At the most, we might make lifelong friends who enrich our lives with their kindness, culture and experience. Quite often, those people may speak different dialects, follow other religions, dress in clothing unlike our own and enjoy diverse cuisines. On occasion, we might feel their lifestyles to be unfamiliar – and we may find ourselves curiously asking questions to broaden our understanding. What builds those connections, however, is the myriad of human conditions that make us all, in fact, very similar. Those deep-rooted emotions of love, joy, fear and pain, that we all feel as human beings, are relatable – no matter where we come from in the world.

Allowing our minds and hearts to be opened to the cultures we encounter – even if that means stepping out of our comfort zone at times – can be a learning curve like no other. It can lead us on an exhilarating emotional journey as well as a physical one, introducing us to different walks of life and inspiring us toward new ways of living. Whatever our experiences while travelling, we must remember that those welcoming us to their homes are also learning about a new culture through our presence. Therefore, it's important for us to tread lightly through the community, and to be a good ambassador for our own society in the process. In this chapter, we delve into the social impact of travel, highlighting the ways in which tourism can affect communities and cultures, and offer solutions on how we, as travellers, can do better. With a fresh perspective and a few small changes to how we approach people and places, we can make tourism a beautiful experience for everyone involved.

TRAVEL ISN'T
ALWAYS PRETTY.
THE JOURNEY
CHANGES YOU; IT
SHOULD CHANGE
YOU. YOU TAKE
SOMETHING WITH
YOU. HOPEFULLY, YOU
LEAVE SOMETHING
GOOD BEHIND.

ANTHONY BOURDAIN

THE SOCIAL IMPACT OF TRAVEL

On the surface of it, tourism seems to bring innumerable social benefits. Yet, if we look more closely at the positives, they are sometimes countered with negative consequences. By understanding that there can be opposing effects from tourism, we can work on what needs changing and strive to be better tourists.

POSITIVES

✓ More income for the region.

✓ More jobs created within the sector.

✓ New infrastructure, such as roads and pipelines, built to accommodate demand.

✓ A market for rental accommodation.

✓ Tourists willing to pay hiked prices to dine locally.

✓ Local customs shared through crafts and performances.

NEGATIVES

✗ The majority of income goes to big chain providers, not communities.

✗ Tourism jobs are typically inconsistent and seasonal, and without security.

✗ Overcrowding and overtourism can devastate current infrastructure.

✗ Local residents are priced out of central locations to make way for Airbnbs and rentals.

✗ Some foods can become unaffordable for the community.

✗ Traditions are modified and westernized to accommodate visitor experiences.

CASE STUDY:

THE TALE OF THE POMPARAN OMPU ONDOL BUTARBUTAR PEOPLE

Idyllic Danau (Lake) Toba in Sumatra, Indonesia, has long been a haunt for the explorative backpacker. The natural waterbody is found in the caldera of a volcano, and is the largest volcanic lake in the world, measuring 100 kilometres (62 miles) long and 30 kilometres (19 miles) wide. Despite its impressive stature, the region doesn't see nearly as many tourists as the popular eastern Indonesian hubs such as Bali and Lombok – so in a bid to draw in more high-end tourists, President Joko Widodo announced plans for a new tourist resort, coinciding with a further nine cross-country "tourism hubs", to rival Bali's popularity.

As a result, members of the Pomparan Ompu Ondol Butarbutar Indigenous community have been threatened with eviction to make room for a proposed five-star hotel, luxury shopping mall, amusement park and golf course. Some people have even found their farms destroyed to ensure they have nothing to tie them to the land. While they have filed lawsuits to keep their ancestral land, their claims are currently unrecognized – their fate sealed by tourism "development".

THE DECOLONIZATION OF TRAVEL AND WHY WE NEED IT

An early colonizer / indigenous community portrayal

*Wherever the European has trod, death seems to pursue
the aboriginal. We may look to the wide extent of the
Americas, Polynesia, the Cape of Good Hope and
Australia and we find the same result...*
Charles Darwin

In early works, native people were often depicted as being primitive savages who fought for their territory but lost to the civilized colonizers. The next traveller accounts followed this narrative, portraying the results of colonization as a "saviour" to the Indigenous communities, who were grateful for the "benefits" of a western lifestyle. With that came a mirror image of western architecture, religion and broad-scale land clearing for farming – features of what colonizers deemed to mean "progression". However, what is rarely shared is the story from an Indigenous population's perspective – that segregation, stolen children, rape and genocide were widespread, and that along with those atrocities came diseases, such as smallpox and measles. Sadly, the impact of those early explorations was far from the romanticized impressions in some history books. Instead, it shaped generations of communities around the world – from Australia to America, Fiji to Mauritius. This is why, to truly appreciate the full story of a place, we should take the time to learn the history from all perspectives.

ACKNOWLEDGING THE BAD

Many of those early voyages of exploration led to colonization, leaving a trail of devastation around the people who already called those lands home. While we may be familiar with the general premise, understanding the specific history behind the places we choose to visit offers valuable context to the people and cultures we come across. If we are honest, not all of it will be pretty. The history of a country – particularly one linked to colonization – can be quite jarring, distressing and even painful to read or hear about. Still, this is the reality of the people who live there and while we shouldn't feel responsible for the actions of those who came before us, it's only right to acknowledge their impact. History, good and bad, has shaped the world we see today. Heritage and consciences are woven together by these events. By being aware of the raw identity of a place and its people, we show respect to those who welcome us. Arguably, this is an essential aspect to fully embracing any travel experience.

CASE STUDY:

THE REAL STORY BEHIND CAPTAIN COOK

Captain James Cook was a British explorer, famous for his voyages to the Pacific Ocean during the late eighteenth century. He is often talked about – and celebrated – for his role in the British colonization of Australia in April 1770. Yet, the notion of Cook "discovering" Australia is a gross misconception. Not only have Indigenous people inhabited this vast continent for over 60,000 years, but other Europeans had already charted various regions – including Dutch navigator Willem Janszoon in 1606 and Englishman William Dampier in 1688. In truth, James Cook simply claimed and named New South Wales for England in 1770. In 1835, the governor of New South Wales, Sir Richard Bourke, issued a proclamation declaring Australia a "terra nullius" or "no man's land". This doctrine meant Indigenous land ownership could be disregarded, that the land belonged to no one and could, therefore, be taken.

UNPICKING THE "COLONIAL CHARM"

Behind the grandeur, architecture and pretty tea terraces, many current and former European colonies have turbulent stories to be told. This history is crucial knowledge when attempting to understand the political and cultural way of life within each country now, in the 21st century. These are just three examples:

SOUTH AFRICA

On arrival in Cape Town in 1652, Dutch traders demanded cattle and labour from the Indigenous Khoikhoi and San populations. When the community refused, the Dutch established agricultural land, bringing in enslaved people from central and west Africa, and India, for labour. Systemic racism remained long after abolition, sanctioning the apartheid era of the twentieth century. The intergenerational trauma continues today.

INDIA

During the colonization of India, the creation of a major trade post allowed the British Crown to transform India's political and social structures. Policies were introduced in the name of reform, but only for Indian communities. This cemented the caste system, marginalizing minority ethnicities, which is still in place.

RWANDA

Pre-colonization, Hutu, Tutsi and Twa ethnicities shared similar beliefs and customs. However, as Belgium took over, Tutsi elites were promoted into power, while non-Tutsi chiefs were rejected. As independence loomed, the policy switched, with Hutus helped into political roles. Rebel groups formed from the fall out, fuelling the 1994 genocide.

TRAVEL THROUGH A HISTORICAL LENS

The urge to travel has always been in our blood. Even the first civilizations were migrating around the world to find suitable environments for their populations to thrive. By the time Europeans were exploring in the fifteenth to eighteenth centuries, they were accompanied by advanced equipment such as chronometers and guns. In those times, travel by sea didn't come with budget options and European explorers needed significant financial backing – and connections – to plan and execute an expedition. At the time, women typically remained at home, running the household and looking after the family, so these travellers were almost always male. For this same reason, many of the first travel journals, scripts and depictions were drafted from the memoirs of one particular demographic: somewhat wealthy, European men. As a result, most of the early perspectives of the world were formed and spread through this same lens. As conscious travellers, we can receive a more rounded perspective by reading historical accounts from authors of varied backgrounds.

THREE POWERFUL FILMS THAT SHARE A DEEPER HISTORY

The remnants of the early-1990s war in Bosnia and Herzegovina still remain in place, most visibly as pock-mark bullet holes in Mostar's old buildings. *Unfinished Business*, a BBC documentary presented by Jeremy Bowen, tells the graphic and heart-breaking story from the time.

Home to jungle wildlife, golden sand beaches and stunning mountain passes, it's easy to understand why Sri Lanka is often labelled as "paradise". *Sri Lanka's Killing Fields*, by the UK's Channel 4, depicts an alternative viewpoint on this teardrop-shaped Indian Ocean island, detailing the atrocities civilians faced during the domestic war.

Beautiful white-sand beaches, rusty-red mountain backdrops and lush vineyards – Australia's brochure-perfect images are hard to resist. *Utopia* by journalist John Pilger tells the story behind Australia Day, the January celebrations that mark when the continent was "founded" by Europeans. To the continent's First Nations people, the day marks violent struggles and loss of life.

CASE STUDY:

BUILDING A MORE POSITIVE FUTURE

While the conversation around acknowledging the good and bad sides of world history grows, the UK's National Trust organization has pledged to be more accurate in its storytelling across its parks, reserves and heritage buildings. Set up in 1895, the Trust is Europe's largest conservation charity, preserving nature and history across woodland, countryside and coastlines. Within those areas are over 500 historic buildings holding diverse collections, including one million works of art. In 2020, the charity released its first ever Colonialism and Historic Slavery report, addressing 93 places and collections that have historical links to the colonial era, including the global slave trade, enslaved labour, abolition and the British Raj in India.

A spokesperson explained, "It's our responsibility to make sure we are historically accurate and academically robust when we communicate about the places and collections in our care." Thanks to this simple acknowledgement, the National Trust now presents its six million members and millions of additional visitors with a sincerer view of British history.

RESPECTING INDIGENOUS LAND

Indigenous cultures all across the world have been forced to accept their land rights being stripped and handed to various industries – from mining and farming to tourism and finance. From Australia to America, the Amazon to the Bornean jungle, when the money calls, native landowners find they have little say in development. Worse still, they are usually poorly compensated – if at all – for their loss. As travellers, we can attempt to relieve some of this trauma by learning the story of these cases before we travel. Then, once in situ, we can make the effort to visit nearby cultural centres – preferably with an Indigenous guide – to learn the situation on the ground. Research will provide details about the landowners or custodians of the region. Again, not all the details will be pleasant, but what matters is to leave with a heart full of understanding for the place and people you've encountered; plus, the income will benefit the community. It's a small gesture, but it can support those at the centre of injustice as they reckon with their history.

CASE STUDY:

CLIMBING ULURU

Inside Uluru-Kata Tjuta National Park, one of Australia's most famous natural monuments – the giant rust-coloured rock known as Uluru – has been attracting tourists since the 1930s. The site is spiritually sacred to the local Anangu community, and for decades, the community have watched on as the local government received sizeable proceeds from tourism. Tens of thousands of tourists are thought to have made the climb each day, veering off established paths for photo opportunities, dropping litter and even defecating around this precious site. Astonishingly, 74 climbers needed medical rescue between 2002 and 2009, and 36 people have died en route. After a long campaign, in October 2019, Northern Territory leaders agreed to close the track for reasons of both safety and cultural respect. The Anangu sign near the entrance now reads, "Please don't climb. This is our home. As custodians, we are responsible for your safety and behaviour."

VOLUNTOURISM A GOOD THING?

The merging of two words – volunteer and tourism – shows just how popular this mode of travelling has become. The idea is to allow travellers to give back to the community they are visiting – but while the thought is kind, the reality can be a little more complex.

Voluntourism typically asks the traveller to sign up to an organized programme – paying a set fee to compensate for their accommodation and meals. Projects include teaching English in primary schools, building houses or classrooms, working in orphanages and assisting at wildlife rehabilitation centres. While the traveller's intent is often steeped in compassion, some agencies take advantage of this thoughtfulness. For example, it's widely known that some Cambodian orphanages hosting voluntourism projects buy or lease children from poverty-stricken parents. As a voluntourist, it's hard to know if we are contributing to such an exploitative business.

ETHICAL VOLUNTEERING

Here are a few ideas on how to give back to communities in a more ethical way.

→ Sign up for projects that align with your skills. For example, only teach English if you are qualified to teach.

→ Choose a programme that teams up with local workers, so your abilities can be used for valuable education.

→ Support programmes that encourage self-development in the community. This way, people can learn to support themselves.

→ It can be heartbreaking to watch children begging on the street, but hold back from handing out cash, which can lead to exploitation. Instead, donate to a homeless shelter or a food bank.

→ Dishing out sweets or soft drinks to children might make them smile, but many don't have regular access to dental care. Consider donating school supplies instead.

→ Ask yourself why you want to help. Is it because you wish to empower vulnerable communities? Or are you hoping for the ultimate social media post? Be honest with yourself and only help for the right reasons.

UNDERSTANDING "WHITE SAVIOURISM" – AND HOW TO AVOID IT

Sometimes travellers find themselves wanting to take a person, or people, they meet under their wing in the hope they can do something good for them. Sponsoring seemingly vulnerable children, teaching in schools, buying gifts, and donating large sums of money to a specific child or family are all ways this can be demonstrated. While these are meaningful gestures that may carry the best of intentions, the reality for the communities on the receiving end is that a stranger from another country, often without suitable qualifications or vetting, is able to take these actions – sometimes without prior consent from the families or children involved. This situation wouldn't be allowed without background checks and consent in our home countries – quite rightly – for reasons of safety and security. In such circumstances, it's worth considering whether our perception that someone needs to be "rescued" is just that – a perception, evoked from the context of our western gaze. As a result, we should carefully consider whether our help is truly needed and of value. People are often motivated to intervene because they imagine they can help to create a better life for someone, but this belief can stem from a lack of understanding about an individual and their culture.

If you decide to offer assistance, be especially careful not to allow unconscious bias to lead your actions. At the same time, avoid placing yourself as the hero of the story – with social media posts and storytelling centred around your actions rather than the wider context. Unfortunately, this narrative projects age-old stereotypes about who are the saviours (largely well-off, western people) and who the helpless people in need of rescuing are (Black and Brown communities). In some situations, the "saviour" might come from a country that, in the past, invaded the region, and caused untold devastation to the generations that came before. In these cases, an offer to help can add insult to injury. Looking at the wider picture is so crucial. It's only natural to want to help, but *how* we do so matters.

GIVING BACK RESPONSIBLY

Caring about issues such as poverty, education, health, women's rights and injustice is a wonderful thing. Here are a few suggestions on how to offer something positive without projecting stereotypes.

→ Choose a community or cause that is close to your heart – someone or something you feel passion for and have read about thoroughly.

→ Engage with the community you're working alongside, get to know them and spend time speaking with them about their lives. It may even take a few return trips before you decide how best to assist.

→ Be sure your desire to help comes from the right place. Do not centre yourself as the problem solver. Instead, be present, listen and focus on the people around you.

→ Work out how to help by asking questions, not by judging what you feel is best.

→ Avoid making grand gestures; keep your efforts small and purposeful.

→ Handing out cash is rarely the solution. Instead, look at what is practically needed.

→ Share donations with community leaders directly, where possible, rather than with international operators.

→ Make useful contributions – educational equipment, books, pens, pencils and notepads are always valuable.

→ If you wish to raise awareness about injustice on social media, do so without images of specific people who don't know their life is being amplified. Images on social platforms can be misconstrued, stereotyped and taken out of context.

→ Rather than tell the story from your point of view, platform important voices of other people in that particular situation.

→ If you choose to support one family or person, do so with discretion, without putting them in the limelight.

→ While it's nice to share your experiences with loved ones, question whether it's necessary to flood social media with photos.

→ If you are compelled to photograph each charitable act for social media to garner praise or raise your own platform, ask yourself what your intentions are.

LETTING GO OF PRECONCEPTIONS

Reading about far-off places you've always dreamed of visiting can conjure up the most enticing images. Take Bali, for instance. With movies such as *Eat, Pray, Love* setting the scene, what do *you* imagine when you dream of Bali? Perhaps it's the scent of sandalwood filling the air, monks strolling to temples wrapped in sunset-coloured robes, retreats built within lush jungles, or frangipani flowers trailing the path to tranquil spas. These picture-perfect depictions are conjugated from social platforms, brochures and modern travel writing. The everyday reality, however, can be quite different – after all, Bali is a living, working environment. Like other parts of the world, motorbikes whizz in and out of standstill traffic. Frangipani grows only in-season, during the spring, and many trees have been cut down to make way for highways. The lesson? Every part of the world moves with the times, and sometimes modernization doesn't conform to romanticized portrayals. So, let's leave behind the stereotypes and visit places with fresh eyes, ready to experience the beauty of real life.

MORE IN COMMON

While modern perspectives aren't as brutal as their colonial counterparts, biases based on unfamiliarity are still found in travel writing today. If we're unaware of these biases when we read travel diaries and articles, we risk furthering prejudices and harmful tropes.

"Exoticism" is typically used in western language to simplify peoples, places and cultures as "foreign", when customs or physical characteristics differ to those of the person commenting.

It's important to understand that, while cultures might be different, we are also very much the same in how we think and feel as human beings – and to truly immerse ourselves in and welcome new experiences, we should endeavour to leave our preconceptions behind. This is a valuable lesson in empathy, compassion and kindness.

CULTURE AS A COMMODITY

Across the world, cultural buildings, performances, artefacts and even traditions, are used to draw in a tourist revenue. In some places, rather than allowing culture to flourish, diversify and develop under its own steam, it is often treated as a commodity – as though it's an item that can be freely bought and sold. As travellers, we have the responsibility to resist treating places as menageries or museums. It's up to us to find – and draw – the line between embracing and enjoying the cultures we come across, and expecting to be entertained. Once again, this comes back to the very first point made in this book: that reframing, in our own minds, how we see the places we visit – a home and secure environment for people, rather than a destination for us – will allow us to respect, absorb and value unfamiliar cultures in the same way we value our own.

EMBRACING CULTURES

Culture consists of learned patterns of thoughts and behaviours that characterize a particular community. It includes language, beliefs, values, traditions and political establishment. Even a little understanding can heighten your travel experience.

→ Read about the culture of the place before you leave. Lonely Planet, Bradt Travel Guides, Rough Guides and National Geographic are all great sources of background information.

→ Get talking to people you meet along the way. There's no better way to dig beneath the surface.

→ Go beyond operator-led experiences. Venture out to popular local hangouts, away from the tourist trail.

→ Take time out to people-watch. It gives you time to process your experiences.

→ Ask questions of local guides to find out about the stories they have to tell.

→ Attend services – go to church, visit the central mosque or light a candle at the temple – wander through cemeteries, explore exhibitions, trawl through libraries and read books by local authors.

BUILDING A RAPPORT

→ **Learn a few words** in the most common local language. "Please", "Thank you", "Hello" and "Goodbye" are good places to start. Carry a phrase book or use Google Translate to help you ask questions, such as "Please may I take your picture?"

→ **Tip directly** if you receive good service. Tourism jobs generally pay employees minimal wages for seasonal work. Tipping helps to make a living wage.

→ **Avoid bartering** at markets to save yourself minimal cash, as the extra money might make a significant difference to the person you're buying from. As a rule, pay what a product is worth.

→ **Carry a sarong or shawl** if you often dress with your shoulders uncovered, in case you end up somewhere that requires conservative clothing. Both will cover shoulders and can be fashioned to cover the upper legs, too.

→ **Avoid tourist-marketed cultural experiences** that put on a superficial show without real insight into the community. Choose to visit local museums and craft markets to learn more and, if you feel safe, say "yes" when people invite you into their homes.

RESPONSIBLE PHOTOGRAPHY

Taking photographs while travelling is a lovely way of documenting a trip – but do bear in mind that snapping pictures isn't a free-for-all. This is most apparent when photographing people, because while intentions might be innocent, photographs can feel invasive to those in front of the lens. As a general rule, the photograph should not be taken unless explicit permission is given by the subject. If you're photographing a crowd, be aware of people's reactions and move on if anyone seems disgruntled. With social media use, extra consideration should be taken with regard to how people are represented. "Poverty porn", for example, refers to media, including personal photographs, that exploits poverty in order to generate sympathy, sales or attention. Such images portray people in a narrative that they have not consented to – yet all too often, travellers snap passing figures who fit their own stereotypical assumption. Before taking the shot, it's worth asking yourself how you might feel if a stranger snapped a picture of you – or your children – in that moment.

CASE STUDY:

FINE FOR A GEISHA

Tourists might be surprised to learn that they can be fined for snapping an unauthorized picture of a Japanese geisha. The fee is (at the time of writing) in place in Gion, a popular district of Kyoto, where it's common to see women dressed in their ceremonial clothing. After decades of tourists abandoning their politeness to take unwarranted shots and sneaky selfies – local residents and shop owners have taken it upon themselves to implement the policy to protect the geishas from invasive behaviour. Now surveillance cameras and warning notices are seen along the streets of Gion, while tourists are handed leaflets detailing the ban. Kyoto is one of Japan's most visited cities and in peak season it can be overcrowded. The Japanese government has responded by launching a tourism campaign packed with suggestions away from the current tourist hubs, with hopes to lighten the load in Kyoto.

HOW TO FEEL MORE COMFORTABLE AT UNFAMILIAR RELIGIOUS EVENTS

Religion is a large part of many people's identity and can be a huge unifier for communities.

→ A quick online search will tell you about any significant dates and events taking place in the region you are visiting.

→ Read a little about the history behind the date, so you know what to expect.

→ Ensure you have packed suitable clothing that follows the customs. If you're unsure of what to wear, or need to buy an outfit, shop in advance of the event and ask a local salesperson to help you.

→ Engage in conversations with your accommodation host or other people you meet along the way; ask questions about the event and its traditions.

→ Consider accepting invitations to attend public celebrations.

→ Enjoy the music, experiment with unfamiliar foods and dance. Immersing yourself at such events is a great way to get to know the people and lifestyles around you.

STEPPING INSIDE SOMEONE'S HOME

If you know basic customs – such as a few words in the local language, how to dress appropriately and any food-related traditions – it's likely you will instantly feel more comfortable in someone else's home. Other ways to settle in include:

→ Bringing a small offering. Alcohol may not always be appropriate, but a dessert often is. If in doubt, simply write a thank you card.

→ Watching how your host acts. If they leave their shoes at the door, do the same. If they aren't walking around with bare feet, put on socks.

→ Offering to help in the kitchen or set the table, rather than expecting to be waited on.

→ Approaching the meal in the same way as your host. If they use a spoon rather than fork, do the same. If they say a prayer beforehand, bow your head for a few seconds.

→ Don't be put off by the unfamiliar. Your host will want you to feel at ease, so try to do exactly that. Their hospitality is a kind gesture, so be yourself and enjoy.

EATING WITH YOUR HANDS

Practised by many cultures around the world, eating by hand is about more than you might realize.

DOWN TO THE ELEMENTS

Veda scriptures, the holy teachings on Hinduism, suggest that the natural elements of space, air, fire, water and earth are evoked by touching food, which prepares the body – and digestive system – for the coming meal.

DEEPER CONNECTIONS

Eating by hand typically means mixing a variety of dishes served on one plate, creating a blend of flavours. The mixing and compiling of a mouthful of food with your own hand opens up a humbling connection with the food.

MINDFUL CONSUMPTION

The nerve endings in your fingertips can feel the texture of the food, sending impulses to the brain to pre-empt flavour and temperature.

REDUCING OVEREATING

Rather than scoff down the meal quickly, eating with your hands slows down the consumption process, allowing your body more time to digest the food as you eat. This encourages your body to feel full sooner.

IT'S EASIER!

For many foods commonly eaten by hand, a knife and fork just wouldn't cut it. Flatbread with pulses, a worldwide staple, is a great example of this.

SUSHI ETIQUETTE

Japanese sushi dishes often take a long time to create, and the process is considered quite an art form. If you visit a restaurant, especially in-country, adopting the following traditions is a lovely way to show respect for Japanese heritage *and* the chef's hard work.

GO GENTLY WITH THE SOY

Dipping your whole sushi into soy sauce or pouring the sauce over the food is considered disrespectful in some restaurants. Instead, use the provided shavings of ginger to gently garnish the sushi with enough soy.

BE CHOPSTICKS AWARE

Avoid sharing food using chopsticks. Evidence from old funerary rituals suggest people used to pass cremated bones using chopsticks, and it is understandably bad luck to evoke this image while eating.

EAT EACH PART OF YOUR BENTO BOWL INDIVIDUALLY

Never mix the ingredients in a Bento bowl (fish, salmon roe, sushi, rice...) – instead, show consideration for the intricate detail of the dish by savouring each part slowly.

RICE IS SACRED

Leaving your chopsticks upright in a rice bowl is considered to be a morbid symbol. If you wish to rest your chopsticks, lay them on the stand provided.

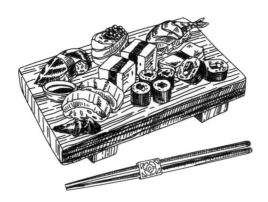

CHAPTER THREE

PLANNING
YOUR
NEXT TRIP

With an understanding of the various ways in which tourism can impact the people and places we visit, we are better equipped to plan a more responsible travel experience. Whether we stay local or go abroad, choose to immerse ourselves in culture or to head into the great outdoors – we now know how to view the places we visit through a lens of mutual respect. The final section of this book offers a detailed and practical guide to planning your next get-away. Not every piece of advice will be relevant for every journey. However, there are a variety of tips and suggestions to consider that will hopefully come in handy on varied occasions. While the advice covers most bases, do still spend time researching your chosen region in greater detail to get the most up-to-date information before you book. Most of all, remember you are planning yet another adventure in this beautiful world, so enjoy the preparation process with the knowledge you are putting together an ethical trip.

NO ONE WILL
PROTECT WHAT
THEY DON'T
CARE ABOUT;
AND NO ONE WILL
CARE ABOUT
WHAT THEY
HAVE NEVER
EXPERIENCED.

**SIR DAVID
ATTENBOROUGH**

RESPONSIBLE TRAVEL – CHOOSING WHERE TO GO

→ Create a list of places that you are excited to travel to, in order of dreaming.

→ Highlight the regions that have already adopted a positive tourism infrastructure. We discussed a few current examples on page 62, but these certainly aren't the only places to enforce sustainable travel measures – so research widely!

→ Cross off anywhere that may be in the midst of any human rights violations or civil unrest, or ruled by dictatorial regimes.

→ If your travels involve flying, calculate your carbon emissions to understand which journeys make less of an impact. Prioritize low-emission routes.

→ Cross off any places that have suffered as a result of travel; for example, overtourism or destruction of natural environments.

→ If your main reason for travel is to experience a wildlife encounter, rule out anywhere that is reported to exploit wildlife.

Now you have a shortlist! The final step is to highlight the places you could reach without getting on a plane. If at all possible, try to make your trip flight-free.

CALCULATE
YOUR EMISSIONS

Use the official carbon calculator by the International Civil Aviation Organization (ICAO) to work out your emissions efficiently.[15]

To get an idea of the amount of carbon emissions you might produce, here are a selection of popular flight routes, with carbon emissions calculated. All examples are return journeys made in economy class. By calculating your emissions before you book, you might be inclined to choose an alternative place to visit or, if possible, another mode of transport.

Route	Distance (km / miles)	CO_2 emissions (kg)/passenger
London – Dublin – London	898 / 558	124.0
London – Marrakech – London	4,586 / 2,850	371.0
New York – London – New York	11,072 / 6,880	621.8
Mumbai – London – Mumbai	14,416 / 8,958	633.8
London – Dubai – London	10,986 / 6,826	689.3
Sydney – Singapore – Sydney	12,578 / 7,816	698.9
Madrid – Buenos Aires – Madrid	20,158 / 12,525	829.3
Sydney – Los Angeles – Sydney	24,112 / 14,983	1,105.8
Amsterdam – Cape Town – Amsterdam	19,358 / 12,029	1,128.0
Melbourne – Doha – Melbourne	23,898 / 14,849.5	1,336.0

If you choose to offset your carbon emissions, follow the steps to more ethical offsetting on page 26.

FIVE SUSTAINABLE OPERATORS

If you choose to book your trip through a travel operator, look out for their policies around sustainable and ethical travel beforehand. These five operators are currently leading the way in more responsible travel...

INTREPID TRAVEL

Taking global small-group tours led by local guides, Intrepid is a certified B Corporation operator – meaning it upholds high standards of social and environmental performance and public transparency. The non-profit Intrepid Foundation works to improve the livelihoods of vulnerable communities through education, skills training, gender equality and job creation.

JORO EXPERIENCES

Another B Corporation with its ethics steeped in responsible travel, UK-based Joro is a founding member of the Conscious Travel Foundation and encourages land-based, flight-free travel. Regular audits take place to keep things in check, while trips are always led by experts, with scientists even sometimes taking the helm.

MUCH BETTER ADVENTURES

Founders of the Tourism Declares a Climate Emergency movement, this operator provides exciting and unforgettable adventures while also investing in reforestation, rewilding and conservation projects around the world. It also collaborates with locally owned businesses to ensure a large slice of tour revenue goes back into communities.

G ADVENTURES

Another company promoting small group tours, G focuses on running ethical experiences that tread lightly in both the community and surrounding environment. Trips range from wellness experiences to marine adventures. The company's "Ripple Score" calculates what percentage of income from each tour stays within the community. G also teams up with ethical partners, such as National Geographic, to offer educational experiences.

LINDBLAD EXPEDITIONS

This expedition cruise line also partners with National Geographic to take a small number of guests to incredible, far-reaching corners of the world – including the Arctic circle and the Antarctic Peninsula. Its primary focus is to provide active, educational tours that teach visitors about environment, wildlife and culture. Its ships push

for sustainability in *all* departments, including the
restaurant where only sustainably and mostly locally
sourced produce is served. Cruises are free of all single-
use plastics.

Use the search engine Ecosia for all your trip research – its
profits go toward planting native trees around the world.

DIVING WITH A PURPOSE

This fantastic non-profit organization, founded by the National Association of Black Scuba Divers and the National Park Service from Biscayne National Park in Florida, supports the conservation of heritage projects around the world, with a primary focus on the African Diaspora. The scheme invites experienced volunteer Scuba divers – including youths – who aspire to learn more about the underwater archaeology associated with the Trans-Atlantic slave trade. It's estimated that 12.5 million people were shipped from the west coast of Africa to America. This programme centres around slave trade shipwreck sites that have, in the past, been looted for their remaining artefacts or are damaged through underwater erosion and the changing environment. Divers learn how to locate, map, document and uncover remaining artefacts from the shipwrecks, providing valuable context to the untold stories of countless enslaved people. To date, around 500 divers have helped to document 18 shipwrecks across six countries.

SLOW TRAVEL: EMBRACING THE JOURNEY

Slow travel refers to the idea of swapping plane trips for overland travel, allowing you to spend more time soaking in and enjoying the journey. This might mean taking trains and buses, hiring an electric or hybrid car for a part of the trip, or even cycling or walking some of the route. Regardless of how you choose to do it, slow travel allows you to make the passage a part of the adventure, giving you time to take in more of the little details as you go. As you get to know the people, food, language and history, you might find you are developing a deeper connection with the place you are exploring.

STUCK FOR TIME?

Of course, taking extra time for a slow travel experience isn't always feasible in the working world, in which case it's worth rethinking how you spread out your annual leave dates. Rather than planning for multiple international trips that increase your carbon footprint, opt for one longer break to enjoy the full experience.

BE A MORE ETHICAL TRAVELLER

By being more thoughtful during the preparation stages of our trip, we can help take the pressure off communities who might already be overwhelmed by tourism. Here are a few small things to incorporate into your planning.

→ Opt to travel during shoulder – or even low – season, to reduce the sheer number of people visiting the region at any one time.

→ Use a region-centric guidebook for research – these provide far more in-depth knowledge and experiences than online forums such as TripAdvisor or Google.

→ Book accommodation outside of central hubs to inject income into less-visited communities. Swap resorts for B&Bs, homestays and guesthouses.

→ Shop in community-run stores; avoid malls, chain and resort shops.

→ Use a local operator who can guide you toward genuine experiences – rather than an international operator who likely won't know the intricacies of local life.

→ Enjoy meals in community-run establishments rather than hotel or government eateries. Inject most of your expenditure into local businesses.

→ Put aside a budget for tips at restaurants, bars and so on, to ensure the community directly benefits from your presence.

TAKE SPECIAL CARE TO FIND OUT IF...

→ You may need to dress more conservatively – covering shoulders and knees in particular – when visiting religious buildings such as churches or mosques, or while out in public spaces. Loose-fitting clothing is appropriate for more religious regions, such as parts of the Middle East, India and Indonesia.

→ The place you're visiting tends to avoid consuming a particular dish or ingredient for religious or cultural reasons. This might mean not eating certain foods, such as beef or pork, for the duration of your stay.

→ Your visit coincides with religious or cultural dates. The month of Ramadan, for example, is observed through fasting, prayer, reflection and community get-togethers, and asks Muslim communities to abstain from eating or drinking between sunrise and sunset. While you needn't follow the same rules, do show courtesy by eating in only tourist-serving establishments or using discretion if eating or drinking in public.

WHAT TO PACK

✓ A huge 73 per cent of clothes produced globally end up as landfill,[16] so forego a pre-trip splurge and take the clothes you already own.

✓ If you must buy clothing, buy second-hand. Stick to items that match easily.

✓ Fill reusable containers with shampoos, conditioners and moisturizers to prevent the need for single-use plastics. Shampoo bars are a great alternative.

✓ If you're planning a beach holiday, buy a chemical-free, reef-friendly sunscreen. Avoid the ingredients oxybenzone and octinoxate, which can be harmful to marine life.

✓ Take swimwear that is appropriate for your cultural surroundings.

✓ Buy holiday reading from independent bookshops: www.bookshop.org, www.hive.co.uk and www.wordery.com are useful if you can't shop in person.

✓ Don't pack wet wipes; instead, use a biodegradable alternative.

✓ Take a mini sewing kit for clothing repairs.

✓ Carry reusable items such as a water bottle, cup, food container and cutlery.

✓ Invest in a portable water purifying system; for example, a Water-to-Go™ bottle or Steripen Aqua.™

Carrying a backpack rather than using a suitcase will help keep your packing minimal.

PACK FOR A PURPOSE

If you do have extra space in your baggage, consider contributing something to a valuable community project. The Pack for a Purpose scheme provides soon-to-be travellers with lists of much-needed products for various community projects around the world. The lists come directly from the project leaders, who understand what is most needed in a particular area. The initiative informs travellers on how to help in a way that directly meets needs.

How to do it in six easy steps:

1. Go to www.packforapurpose.org
2. Select the place to which you are travelling.
3. Locate a tour operator or accommodation facility that supports a community project.
4. Choose which supplies you wish to take from the provided list.
5. Pack the items in your baggage.
6. Drop off your supplies at the operator office or accommodation facility who will deliver your items to the project.

Travellers have offered over 202,800 kilograms (446,160 pounds) of supplies via Pack for a Purpose, providing essential needs in over 60 countries.

BETTER TRAVEL INSURANCE PROVIDERS

Some insurance policies are more ethical than others. Here's what to watch out for when choosing a provider.

IS THE COMPANY TRANSPARENT ABOUT ITS INVESTMENTS?

Shareholdings are one way of deciphering the integrity of a company. For example, if it invests in fossil fuels or coal mining in the midst of a climate crisis, its ethics aren't commendable.

IS IT A MEMBER OF CLIMATEWISE?

Companies that register with this voluntary climate-focused initiative commit to supporting climate awareness, informing public policy and reconsidering investment strategy in line with better climate guidelines.

DOES IT PAY TAXES?

As in many lucrative industries, tax avoidance can be rife in the insurance sector. If the company registers its businesses in known tax havens, the chances are it has adopted tax avoidance strategies.

TRY THESE COMPANIES...

✓ ETA – founded by environmentalists and supportive of sustainable transport initiatives.

✓ Naturesave – 10 per cent of premiums go to the Naturesave Trust.

✓ battleface – works with social projects, including the international not-for-profit organization Kiva.

Always do your own research before choosing an insurance company – you should be happy with the company's policies and reputation before spending your money.

TRAVELLING FOR BUSINESS?

Here are a few ways in which you, and your company, can embrace sustainability.

1. USE TECHNOLOGY TO YOUR ADVANTAGE

The Covid-19 pandemic taught us we can work remotely and still be productive. Software such as Zoom, Google Meet or Microsoft Teams is useful for meetings and conferences and a handy alternative to in-person get-togethers.

2. FIND AN ALTERNATIVE TO FLYING

As we know, flying contributes 2 to 3 per cent to the world's greenhouse gas emissions, so choosing to travel regularly by train, coach or rideshares, makes a big difference.

3. SUBSIDIZE THE COMMUTE

If you often drive into work, consider asking your company to contribute toward an annual rail pass – so you can stop commuting by car.

4. PARTNER WITH LOCALLY RUN ACCOMMODATION

This is a great opportunity to support small businesses – such as B&Bs and guesthouses. Consider booking with the same business if you travel there regularly.

5. ENCOURAGE SUSTAINABLE PRACTICE

Offer to plan food and drink for conferences. Focus on investing in reusable equipment and ensuring there are no single-use plastics and as little food waste as possible.

PLANET-FRIENDLY AIRPORT HACKS

Domestic and international airport experiences can be quite stressful. This basic guide to getting to the gate, with minimal fuss and a few sustainable travel options thrown in, should help lighten the load on the day.

→ Download your ticket and boarding pass and any other important travel documentation to your phone or tablet rather than carrying reams of paperwork. Save passes to your "e-wallet" for ease of use.

→ Avoid using the plastic-wrap baggage service at the airport and invest in a padlock instead.

→ Carry an empty reusable water bottle – but don't fill it up until you are past security. Remember: some airports have two security checks.

→ Reduce plastic waste further by packing a sandwich or fruit from home. Eat it, or dispose of it, before disembarking from your flight, and always adhere to biosecurity guidelines.

→ Invest in headphones so you don't need the plastic headsets provided onboard.

→ If you're intending to buy duty-free products for your journey, ensure you have room in your hand luggage first to avoid picking up plastic carrier bags.

OUT IN THE FIELD

→ Wash as efficiently as possible. Avoid baths and long showers, particularly if you're somewhere where water is scarce.

→ Turn off the lights and air-conditioning before you leave your room. Better still, don't use the air conditioning at all and prop open a window instead.

→ Armed with your own reusable water bottle, food container and cutlery, you shouldn't need single-use containers from food and drink vendors. That small action, across your entire trip, saves a significant amount of paper and plastic.

→ If you're out for the day, and not anticipating eating at a café or restaurant, consider buying food from a local market rather than a supermarket.

→ Plan when to stop for meals so you're not running hungry and enticed by snack packages.

→ Carry a small washable bag that can be used for rubbish if you can't find a bin.

→ Honour any reservations to the best of your ability. If you must cancel, let the accommodation or restaurant know well in advance.

TRANSPORT GOALS – ASPIRE TO KEEP YOUR CARBON FOOTPRINT LOW

CITY WALKING TOURS

From New York to Ho Chi Minh, local guides provide highly informative walking tours through segments of the city – usually focusing on a specific subject or cultural aspect. Ask your accommodation hosts for recommendations and learn on foot!

CYCLING AROUND

Bicycle hire is becoming increasingly prevalent in cities and rural areas, offering travellers the opportunity and the independence to explore off the beaten track. Download a map at your accommodation to pre-plan the route you wish to take.

LOCAL BUS

For cross-town trips, consider taking a local bus as it's faster than walking – and it will mean you have more time to explore. Find out beforehand whether you need a pre-paid card to travel (a lot of companies no longer take cash).

TRAINS

Long distance journeys by rail can be exhilarating and relaxing – and often take the same amount of time, door to door, as a domestic flight would. The bonuses are that you're not strapped in and the scenery is more interesting.

PHOTOGRAPHY OF PEOPLE AND PLACES

While landscapes and scenery are easier to manage, photographing people and culture requires more care. These five tips are the baseline for ethical photography:

1. ASK PERMISSION

Carry a phrase book or use Google Translate so you can address the person in their language. Don't take the photo if you're unsure of the answer.

2. MAINTAIN AWARENESS

If you feel uncomfortable, the chances are your subject is feeling the same. Don't force the situation if it doesn't feel right.

3. SHOW GRATITUDE

Share the image afterward, either on the camera screen or by offering to send them the photograph.

4. NEVER PHOTOGRAPH CHILDREN WITHOUT PERMISSION

Always be safe and considerate if you wish to take a photograph of a child. Ensure you have consent from them and their guardian.

5. BE AWARE OF LAWS AND CUSTOMS AROUND PHOTOGRAPHY

Some government buildings, religious figures, monuments and private land aren't permitted to be photographed. Respect those customs, no matter how iconic the scene.

TIPPING ETIQUETTE

Tipping someone who does you a service is a traditional way of showing gratitude. Generally, there isn't a hard and fast rule when it comes to tipping; however, most countries do encourage the gesture to complement the wages of service staff.

AMERICA

Service industry staff in the US are notoriously paid very little and depend on tips to make a living. As a rule, a 10 per cent tip means you were unsatisfied, 15 per cent suggests the service was okay, 20 per cent indicates they did a good job and 25 per cent says your experience was outstanding.

MOROCCO

While tipping is not customary, rounding up to the nearest dirham is standard practice for Moroccans.

BARBADOS

It's generally customary to leave a 10 to 15 per cent tip depending on your satisfaction. This includes restaurants, tour guides and drivers.

AUSTRALIA

In complete contrast to the US, service staff here are generally paid well – so tipping is not expected.

UNITED KINGDOM

The traditional 10 per cent tip etiquette across England, Northern Ireland, Scotland and Wales includes all service industries, from cafés to hairdressers.

If in doubt, give at least 10 per cent.

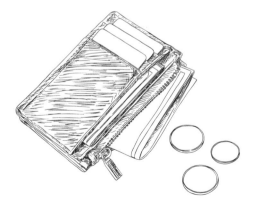

BE SOUVENIR SAVVY

When it comes to shopping, it's easy to get carried away. Keep this list handy for when you're absorbed in perusing.

→ Avoid mass-produced products typically found around the tourist hubs, stations and airports. Instead, seek out smaller-scale artisan markets, handicraft stores and even workshops, where you can buy souvenirs produced by genuine local artists.

→ Avoid bartering with the store owner to grab a bargain, and instead be willing to pay for what a product is worth. To invest in the work of local creatives is a positive contribution.

→ If you're unsure of what to buy but want to support local industry, choose an experience-led investment instead by visiting an exhibition or gallery. Donations are another way to express support.

→ Rather than buying someone back home a gift that may never get used, let them enjoy a more immersive experience from your trip – perhaps by cooking them a local dish or framing a beautiful photograph.

→ Only buy what you can fit into your bags. Remember, heavy luggage contributes to increased transport emissions.

SAY "NO" TO ANIMAL PRODUCTS

Souvenirs made from animal products should be avoided at all costs – even if the region you're in is famed for products crafted from animal skin, teeth or bone. By buying such products, you could be encouraging unhealthy and cruel practices that see animals as a commodity. Occasionally, in tourist-frequented places, locals turn to such merchandise to help make their living. Sadly, in areas where education is low and the importance of wildlife is not understood, animals are often attacked to produce those products. Reptiles, turtles and walrus are just three animals that suffer greatly from such business. In the past, gorilla and orangutan hands were considered valuable gifts. It's up to all of us to say we are not interested in paying money for such products. In addition, many countries – rightly – do not allow you to bring animal products across borders. To find out more about the rules, read about the Convention on International Trade in Endangered Species of Wild Fauna and Flora (CITES).

FIVE WILDLIFE CONSERVATION PROGRAMMES TO SUPPORT

In the US, **The Sierra Club** develops initiatives for local involvement in wildlife preservation. It is also working toward renewable energy sources and fossil fuel alternatives.

Oceanswell in Sri Lanka offers outreach programmes to community members who wish to learn more about marine life. It runs a marine conservation field course and teaches budget building and grant-writing.

Investing public donations into funding, the **Dian Fossey Gorilla Fund** organizes scientific research, the education of surrounding communities on conservation and the protection of mountain gorillas against poaching.

Amazon Watch works with Indigenous populations to preserve the biodiversity in the rainforests of South America.

Across the African continent, **Tusk** works to protect endangered species, tackle the illegal wildlife trade and empower communities to preserve ecosystems and habitats.

Did you know Indigenous people make up 5 per cent of the world's population, but their homelands hold 80 per cent of its biodiversity?[17]

BECOME A
CITIZEN SCIENTIST

From wildlife surveys to environmental studies, citizen science projects allow you to contribute to collaborative volunteer research so that large amounts of data can be collected and studied. If you love being outside and around nature or wildlife, there are so many surveys to get involved with. Earthwatch Europe's WaterBlitz project, for example, uses volunteer data to uncover which inland waterways are suffering from pollution across the continent. On scheduled weekends throughout the year, members are encouraged to use an Earthwatch water testing kit to collate data. You could carry out the test near home – or while travelling if the weekend coincides with your plans. Either way, citizen science projects promote an ethos of "the more, the merrier"; everyone is included and welcome to join in. This can also be a great way to involve children and teach them to be more considerate to the environment around them.

DOWNLOAD THE APPS

→ The iNaturalist app links you with over 400,000 naturalists and scientists and helps you to identify plant and animal species. Scientists then analyze the data for research purposes.

→ The Happywhale project encourages ecotourists to submit photographs of their whale encounters for identification by marine experts. If the whale isn't registered, your image is checked and added to the database. You can then follow its route around the world.

→ The eBird app allows casual and dedicated birdwatchers to register their sightings, including when, where and how they went birding. You can also keep a checklist of all the birds you've seen and heard. Experts then analyze the data patterns.

→ NASA's GLOBE Observer is an international network of scientists (both citizen and professional) working together to learn more about the changing climate. Examples of observations include clouds, land cover, trees and mosquito habitats.

→ Eye on the Reef asks day trippers, tourists and fishers to Australia's Great Barrier Reef to register their observations through the dedicated app. Marine scientists then track changes along the 2,300-kilometre (or 1,429-mile) marine ecosystem.

TO STAYCATION OR NOT TO STAYCATION?

Many people who love to travel have a natural habit of dreaming of far-off destinations. Yet, if there is one positive thing that came out of the Covid-19 pandemic, it's the realization of just how wonderful our own surroundings can be. Planning an escape in your own back yard (so to speak) has become much more popular in recent years – and while much of this happened out of necessity, many of us can agree it's worked out for the best. Why? Because there are so many beautiful and interesting places to explore within our own countries that allow us to travel without causing so many carbon emissions. So next time you're craving a break, consider staying locally over an international trip. By cutting down on multiple international journeys to, say, one trip abroad annually – or better still, once every two years – and opting for domestic travel during those other occasions, you will greatly reduce your carbon footprint. This is an excellent option for anyone who is serious about being a more responsible traveller.

BE A HAPPY (AND SUSTAINABLE) CAMPER

Camping allows you to immerse yourself in nature, away from the stresses of everyday life. Whether you choose to swim, forage, go for a hike or bike ride, read, bird-watch or stargaze – these simple tips will help the process.

→ Rent or borrow tents, sleeping bags, a camping stove and inflatable mattresses if you don't own them.

→ Set up camp away from ground vegetation and on naturally clear ground.

→ Carry enough water and food in a cooler box to be self-sufficient. Avoid single-use plastics.

→ Planning meals in advance will avoid waste. Vegetables, fruit, soups and pasta last well without refrigeration.

→ Wash dishes, and hair, at least 100 metres (or 330 feet) away from a water source.

→ Carry enough biodegradable bin bags for waste and recycling.

→ Bring a trowel for a homemade toilet (at least 60 metres or 200 feet from a water source) and remember to bury everything, including toilet paper, *at least* 15 centimetres (six inches) down.

→ Take any non-compostable rubbish home with you.

→ Use chemical-free sunscreen, especially if wild swimming or bathing in natural water.

TRAVEL AND SOCIAL MEDIA

Unfortunately, in recent years, the need to document and share travel adventures on social media has contributed to the spread of misinformation, prejudice, overtourism and exploitation of people, cultures and the environment. As seasoned travellers, we have a responsibility to do better. Here are a few things to consider before posting.

OVERALL RESPONSIBILITY

→ Travel experiences aren't always perfect, so avoid portraying them as such. Speak honestly about what you've encountered on your journey.

→ Be true to the reality of the place in your post. Pictures don't always tell the whole story, so responsibly share the background or history in the caption.

→ If you are posting about a person or group of people who have given you permission to share their image, take the time to represent them correctly.

→ Some places of significance, including religious monuments, don't allow photographs to be taken. Beware of such rules and don't post any images that contravene them.

ENVIRONMENT AND WILDLIFE

→ If you find yourself in a lesser-known place, do not use a geotag. Share experiences without naming specific locations.

→ Keep on designated tracks or paths to get a picture – by veering off course, you could be damaging soil, crops or other vegetation.

→ *Do* document your ethical practices when encountering wildlife and highlight responsible operators.

→ Never share images of irresponsible tourism practices, such as cub petting or playing with dolphins.

PEOPLE AND CULTURE

→ Publicizing children's identities and locations can leave them vulnerable to crime.

→ Remember: other people's homes are not a traveller's zoo, refrain from posting intimate details about people's private property.

→ If you're posting about a specific issue or injustice, platform the voices at the centre of the injustice if possible.

→ If in doubt, ask yourself how comfortable you would be if a stranger shared a similar image of you.

BECOME AN AMBASSADOR

One of the brilliant things about truly getting to know a place is that it can capture your heart. Once it does, you'll find yourself invested in the environment and the welfare of its people. Use that interest and concern to do something positive – share your awareness with others. If there is an issue that affects the region, its people, environment or wildlife then spend time researching it even further once you get home – and discuss what you've found with those around you. This is also a positive way to action your social media platforms – to educate others on the issues you have explored along the way. In addition, speak up about the places that can do better. Send feedback emails to the businesses you visited, either thanking them for their contribution to a more ethical way of life – or by highlighting greenwashing agendas that were less impressive and need more work. Doing so holds those businesses accountable for their actions, and hopefully helps them to realize change is being demanded from their own clients.

AN EXAMPLE OF TOURIST AMBASSADORSHIP

After an expedition voyage to Antarctica, travellers tend to return home with more awareness of how climate change is affecting polar regions, its ecosystems and wildlife. Whether they witness the thousands-strong penguin colonies that depend on cool temperatures to survive or see the giant icebergs, carved from a mighty Antarctic ice shelf, drifting in the middle of the Southern Ocean – seeing nature happen in front of you, first-hand, is the most heart-jolting of ways to understand the impact of greenhouse emissions. This in-person education can encourage manageable changes in tourists' daily lives – such as the recycling of plastics, supporting conservation projects and, most importantly, an active reduction in their carbon footprint. Just one trip can make you an ambassador for an entire region – and through talking about what you have learned, you may even inspire a change in others. Wherever you choose to visit, you too can become an ambassador.

THE RISE OF THE ARMCHAIR TRAVELLER

For those who are keen to explore the world, but are aware of their environmental and social impact, armchair travel is a superb option for finding escapism without having to leave the comfort of your sofa. The Covid-19 pandemic saw the launch of many incredible virtual experiences, allowing anyone to explore the regions of the world that have long enticed them. Even better, virtual travel experiences allow you to visit the most famous places on the planet without contributing to overtourism – now, *that's* a brilliant bonus.

While it is, of course, not the same as travelling in person, armchair travel is a unique opportunity to see the places we dream of without impacting the surrounding environment and community. See it as a means of witnessing those busier regions – and then make real-life plans to travel to lesser-visited places.

→ Explore Macchu Picu – Google's Street View allows anyone to step right into this scared Peruvian site at the touch of a button.

→ The Louvre Palace in Paris, the former home of the kings of France, offers virtual tours around its vast and glorious museum.

→ www.explore.org's live webcam footage takes you to the depths of several savannahs across the African continent, providing a subtle insight into the lives of the wildlife.

→ Google's Street View takes you to the heart of the Egyptian Pyramids with 360° views over Giza and more.

→ AirPano's incredible panoramic views of Victoria Falls from the sky – presented with some key facts – is a sight to behold.

→ Take a 360° virtual look around The Vatican Museum in Rome and enjoy a frontline view in every room – including the splendid Sistine Chapel.

→ Lights Over Lapland allows you to watch in wonder as the Northern Lights, or Aurora, light up the sky over the Abisko National Park in Sweden.

A FINAL THOUGHT

As consumers of travel and tourism, we are encouraged to prioritize our individual needs over the bigger picture for the planet – but in a world of nearly eight billion people, our environmental and social impact isn't inconsequential. So, perhaps the key to doing better is by changing our role as consumers. Acknowledging that although we have the means to travel, it doesn't mean we always need to, is an important part of the process. Of course, travel is, for so many of us, a way of life – and for those who love to explore, the exhilarating feeling that comes with that freedom will never leave our veins. Yet, if we – the more regular travellers – can combine small lifestyle changes, such as eating less meat or reducing our energy consumption at home, with flying a little less and investing in longer, more in-depth adventures, we can still reap the sweet rewards of travel, while also doing our very best for Planet Earth.

As humanity steps up to tackle the climate emergency and injustice around the world, perhaps we can also make changes to the way in which we act while travelling, so that we too can contribute to a healthier, more stable world. While it's true that the industry as a whole must adapt, we can drive change through our choices – showing the decision makers that we, as travellers, *want* genuinely sustainable and ethical measures to be put into practice. Hopefully this book has provided you with the desire and the tools to become a more responsible traveller, along with the knowledge to help you explore this incredible world with care for the environments around you and compassion for the people you meet along the way. With a few small changes and a more conscious outlook, together we can find a way to preserve our beautiful planet for the generations to come.

RESOURCES

If this book has inspired you to explore the world in a more responsible and ethical way, the following resources are a great place to continue your journey.

GENERAL READING

→ Diamond, Jared *Guns, Germs & Steel: A Short History of Everybody for the Last 13,000 Years* (1998, Vintage)

→ Downing, Elise *Coasting: Running Around the Coast of Britain – Life, Love and (Very) Loose Plans* (2021, Summersdale)

→ Hart, Anna *Departures: A Guide to Letting Go, One Adventure at a Time* (2018, Sphere)

→ Hughes, Robert *The Fatal Shore* (1987, The Harvill Press)

→ Jemil, Nori *The Travel Photographer's Way: Practical Steps To Taking Unforgettable Travel Photos* (2021, Bradt Guides)

→ Lavery, Brian *A Short History of Seafaring* (2019, Dorling Kindersley)

→ Marshall, Tim *Prisoners of Geography: Ten Maps That Tell You Everything You Need to Know About Global Politics* (2016, Elliott & Thompson)

→ Moore, Peter *Swahili for the Broken-Hearted: Cape Town to Cairo By Any Means Possible* (2003, Bantam)

→ Vincent, Jessica; Wood, Levison; Rajesh, Monisha; Willmore, Simon (eds) *The Best British Travel Writing of the 21st Century* (2022, Summersdale)

→ Winn, Raynor *The Salt Path* (2019, Penguin)

CULTURE AND THE ENVIRONMENT

→ Bregman, Rutger *Humankind: A Hopeful History* (2020, Little Brown and Company)

→ Diski, Jenny *Stranger on a Train: Daydreaming and Smoking Around America with Interruptions* (2004, Virago)

→ Flyn, Cal *Islands of Abandonment: Life in the Post-Human Landscape* (2021, William Collins)

→ Hussain, Tharik *Minarets in the Mountains: A Journey into Muslim Europe* (2021, Bradt Travel Guides)

→ Juan, Li *Winter Pasture: One Woman's Journey with China's Kazakh Herders* (2021, Minedition)

→ Pasquale, Maria *How to Be Italian* (2021, Smith Street Books)

→ Rajesh, Monisha *Around the World in 80 Trains: A 45,000-Mile Adventure* (2019, Bloomsbury Publishing)

→ Stewart, Pip *Life Lessons From the Amazon* (2021, Summersdale)

- → Teller, Matthew *Nine Quarters of Jerusalem: A New Biography of the Old City* (2022, Profile Books)
- → Wallace-Wells, David *The Uninhabitable Earth: A Story of the Future* (2019, Allen Lane)

DOCUMENTARIES AND TV SERIES

- → *An Inconvenient Truth* by Al Gore, directed by Davis Guggenheim (2006)
- → *A Life on Our Planet* narrated by Sir David Attenborough (2020, Netflix)
- → *Almost Australian* by Miriam Margoyles (2021, BBC)
- → *Chasing Coral* by Jeff Orlowski (2017, Netflix)
- → *Grizzly Man* by Werner Herzog (2005)
- → *Happy People: A Year in the Taiga* by Dmitry Vasyukov and Werner Herzog (2010)
- → *Jiro Dreams of Sushi* by David Gelb (2011)
- → *Life In a Day: Around the World in 80,000 Clips* directed by Kevin Macdonald (2011)
- → *March of the Penguins* narrated by Morgan Freeman (2005)
- → *My Octopus Teacher* by Craig Foster, Pippa Ehrlich and James Reed (2020, Netflix)
- → *Planet Earth* narrated by Sir David Attenborough (2006, BBC)

- → *Sharkwater* by Rob Stewart (2006)
- → *Stephen Fry in America* (2008, BBC)
- → *The Act of Killing* by Joshua Oppenheimer and Christine Cynn (2012)
- → *Walking The Nile* with Levison Wood (2015, Channel 4)

PODCASTS

- → **The Thoughtful Travel Podcast** with Amanda Kendle combines stories from around the globe with practical advice on how to be a better traveller.
- → The UK's Channel 4 News presenter Krishnan Guru-Murthy and guests delve into the way we think and live in **Ways To Change The World.**
- → **Radio Garden** broadcasts 24 hours of live music from around the world, allowing you to explore the globe through tens of thousands of stations dedicated to the arts.
- → British travel writer Pip Jones hosts the **Travel Goals Podcast**, which invites top travel experts to discuss industry developments and tales from around the world.
- → Journalist and author Aaron Miller's **Armchair Explorer** documentary-style format shares the extraordinary stories of well-known explorers and adventurers.

→ **Women Who Travel** is hosted by the editors of Condé Nast Traveler (US) and discusses a whole host of experiences from women travellers across the world.

→ Author Peter Moore invites fellow travellers and travel experts to share hilarious encounters from around the world in his podcast, **No Shitting in the Toilet**.

ABOUT THE AUTHOR

Karen Edwards is a senior editor and writer from London, who specializes in responsible tourism and sustainable living. She contributes to a variety of national and international titles, including *High Life* by British Airways, *Balance, Breathe, Grazia, The Independent* and *Time Out,* and she currently lives in London with her marine biologist fiancé. Karen inherited her love for the planet at a young age, inspired while exploring with her parents. Since then, she's been fortunate to visit many regions around the world – getting to know environments and communities for her own inquisitive nature and the stories she writes. However, over time and through a lot of learning, Karen's outlook on travel has changed. While finding healing on the road, she also witnessed the effects of the changing climate in Antarctica, the hounding of wildlife in Kenya, overtourism in Thailand and coral bleaching in the Pacific Ocean. She soon realized that a more responsible outlook when travelling is needed, and that planning with care makes the experience all the more rewarding. This is how the idea for this book was born.

REFERENCES

1   International Air Transport Association (IATA)

2   www.sciencedirect.com/science/article/pii/S1352231020305689

3   www.ipcc.ch/sr15

4   WWF arcticwwf.org/work/climate

5   discoveringantarctica.org.uk/oceans-atmosphere-landscape/atmosphere-weather-and-climate/climate-change-past-and-future

6   The Impact of Sea Level Rise and Climate Change on the Pacific Ocean Atolls, US National Climate Change Assessment, 2012 www.usgs.gov/centers/pcmsc/science/impact-sea-level-rise-and-climate-change-pacific-ocean-atolls?qt-science_center_objects=0#qt-science_center_objects

7   www.bbc.co.uk/news/science-environment-49349566

8   Which? Travel, 'Carbon labelling', September 2021

9   www.theguardian.com/environment/ng-interactive/2019/jul/19/carbon-calculator-how-taking-one-flight-emits-as-much-as-many-people-do-in-a-year

10 www.thelocal.es/20190606/barcelona-and-palma-
ranked-worst-in-europe-for-cruise-ship-pollution

11 www.barcelona.cat/metropolis/en/contents/tourism-
between-wealth-and-residents-complaints

12 www.nationalgeographic.com/culture/article/100-
million-sharks-killed-every-year-study-shows-
on-eve-of-international-conference-on-shark-
protection?loggedin=true

13 www.sharkwater.com/help-save-sharks/sharkfree

14 www.tourism-review.com/bali-water-crisis-caused-
by-tourism-news3376

15 www.icao.int/environmental-protection/
Carbonoffset/Pages/default.aspx

16 www.weforum.org/agenda/2019/02/how-the-
circular-economy-is-redesigning-fashions-future

17 www.nationalgeographic.com/environment/
article/can-indigenous-land-stewardship-protect-
biodiversity-

Have you enjoyed this book?
If so, why not write a review on your favourite website?

If you're interested in finding out more about
our books, find us on Facebook at Summersdale
Publishers, on Twitter at @Summersdale and
on Instagram at @summersdalebooks and
get in touch. We'd love to hear from you!

Thanks very much for buying this Summersdale book.

www.summersdale.com